Sew *with* *the* Stars

Sew for the Cure®
a fundraiser for
breast cancer
research

The Sew for the Cure® registered trademark is owned by the Susan G. Komen Breast
Cancer Foundation and is used under license by the Home Sewing Foundation.

www.pbtex.com

SEW WITH THE STARS
© 2002 by P&B Textiles

Editor: Julie Scribner
Technical Editor: Cyndi Hershey
Second Technical Editor: Stevii Graves
Copy Editor: Peggy Kass
Second Copy Editor: Tara Joffe
Graphic Designer: Staci Harpole, Cubic Design
Illustrator: Richard Sheppard
Photographer: Sharon Risedorph
Cover Design: Erica Joy Riggs

Published by P&B Textiles, 1580 Gilbreth Road,
Burlingame, CA 94010

ISBN 0-9713990-0-1

Distributed by Checker Distributors

Printed in China

To Life

YOU CAN MAKE A BID FOR LIFE

The goal of Sew for the Cure® is to raise a million dollars for breast cancer research. Besides the profits from this book, ten of the original quilts and the quilt label will be auctioned online, with all profits going toward this fundraising effort.

If you are interested in owning one of these quilts, or know someone else who might be, please visit our web site, pbtex.com, in the fall of 2002 for details on the auction. You can make a bid for life.

You can send additional donations directly to Sew for the Cure®. Please make out your check to the Home Sewing Foundation, and mail it to HSF at 1350 Broadway, Suite 1601, New York, NY 10018. Please mark "Sew with the Stars" on your check. Thank you for your generosity.

S T A M P   I T   O U T   *By JoAnn Gilbert, Jenny Sloan and Marcia Yates*

Cancer has touched and will touch all of us in our lifetimes in one way or another. Breast cancer research is not about death, but about surviving and about the hope that the research instills in all of us touched by it, whether through personal experience or those we know who have personal experience.

"Inspired by the breast cancer stamp, we obtained permission from the U.S. Postal Service to use the design, and we made the quilt. Marcia and JoAnn worked on the layout; JoAnn pieced it together and sewed on the black outline. Jenny quilted it and finished the binding. We were thrilled with the end result and hope that others will be as well."

JoAnn

"I have been touched by cancer, losing my husband to this insidious disease. I have supported breast cancer research with donations, but I wanted to do something different to help. This form of cancer threatens women all over the world, and no one is immune. Making a quilt from the breast cancer stamp with Jenny and Marcia has been an uplifting experience for me and hopefully will inspire others not to give up hope."

Jenny

"Even though I have no family history of breast cancer, I am very much aware of how this affects those who do have it. It is such an evil disease. This project was a group effort from start to finish. We were inspired by the cause, the quilt, and by each other."

Marcia

"I am proud to have worked together with two wonderful artists on a piece of art that represents the hope for all of us; our mothers, sisters, aunts, daughters, and all our female relations."

Note: The U.S. Postal Service did not give us permission to print a pattern of this quilt for this book.

Foreword

This book is about love. There is hope for a cure for breast cancer. Although there is an increase in the reported cases of breast cancer annually, there is a decrease in the mortality rate. This drop is due in great part to improved research and treatment. This is the trend we want to nurture, and that is what this book supports. All of these original patterns and quilts have been donated by the quilt makers. All wholesale profits from this book will go to the Home Sewing Association's Sew for the Cure® fundraising campaign. Proceeds are donated to the American Cancer Society, the National Alliance of Breast Cancer Organizations and the Susan G. Komen Foundation. By purchasing this book, you are personally contributing to an important cause, and helping to find a cure for the sake of all of us and for future generations. Although it is predominantly a woman's disease, the effects of breast cancer on all family members make it a critical concern for everyone.

The love that you have for quilting can help continue the vital research needed to eliminate this global health issue. Merely by enjoying your creation of the quilts in this book, you are sustaining the research that will lead to a cure. In the same way that you sow love by giving a quilt to a family member or friend, you propagate love worldwide by supporting the eradication of this illness. Your passion will soothe and heal the world in more ways than one, and in a more universal manner than you ever could have imagined. Thank you for participating.

Julie Scribner, *Editor*

The Home Sewing Association is the sole organization representing the entire home sewing industry. The Association's mission is two-fold: to foster the development of sewing skills and inspire increased consumer sewing activity; and to promote the growth of the home sewing industry and HSA members by providing vehicles for education, marketplace development, public relations, idea exchange and profitable business relationships.

Acknowledgements

There are many people who have given of their time, talent and knowledge to participate in the production of this book and bring it to fruition. First and foremost, we thank the quilters, without whom there would be no book. Their dedication to this cause is evident in the beautiful projects they have created from their hearts and donated as a part of themselves.

We also extend our sincere gratitude to Rob Kreiger and the staff of Checker Distributors, who donated their distribution services to bring this book to you. Thanks to Sharon Risedorph for donating her photography services on all the quilt projects.

Our thanks go out to Todd Hensley and the staff of C&T Publishing, who gave us so much advice and support on our first book venture.

Thanks to Cyndi Hershey, our merchandise consultant, who spent countless hours proofreading the technical part of the book. Thanks also to the following people: to Stevii Graves and Tara Joffe, who donated their editing services; to Donna Pierson and the staff of the Home Sewing Association for their collaboration and support on this project; and to Deborah Corsini, our former design director, for pulling all the quilters into this project. The journey would have been much more difficult without all of these people.

Finally, my deepest appreciation to Julie Scribner, our marketing director, who, while learning her new job, was the group leader who made it all come together.

Irwin Bear
President, P&B Textiles
Chairman, Sew for the Cure®

Contents

With Heart and Hand

"Years ago, a tall oak tree fell on me in a car stopped at a red light. Family, friends and people whose names I never knew pitched in with childcare and casseroles, carpools and co-op babysitting chits. When I fretted that I could never repay each kindness, my neighbor explained, 'When you are in need, folks help. When someone else is in need and you are able, you help.' The good fortune of that accident is that it has left me a lifetime of repaying to do. So I thank Irwin for allowing me to be a part of his P&B Textiles community and a part of this breast cancer fundraising book. I hope it helps someone in need."

By Elly Sienkiewicz ◆ Utilizing the *Baltimore Beauties III* collection
Finished size: 8 ³/₄" x 11¹/₂"

Elly

Elly Sienkiewicz is widely credited with fueling the late 20th century Baltimore Album Quilt revival, which continues into the 21st century. She has written fifteen needlework books, including the series of ten Baltimore Beauties® books, which began in 1989. She has her own applique school, the Elly Sienkiewicz Applique Academy in Williamsburg, Virginia. In 1999, the group quilt she designed and brought to life, "The Good Ladies of Baltimore," was chosen one of the Hundred Best Quilts of the Twentieth Century. Elly has created three collections for P&B Textiles, each based on authentic patterns from the late 19th century, that were used in Baltimore Album Quilts. Now a stitching grandmother, Elly lives in Washington, DC, with her husband Stan.

BALTIMORE BEAUTIES III COLLECTION
by Elly Sienkiewicz

Elly styled several fabric collections for P&B Textiles with the Baltimore Album Quilt form in mind. This group offers an abundance of florals in rich, classic colors. The look is old-fashioned, and the patterns are derived from antique swatches and illustrations, some of which have been changed or embellished for the collection. Most are from the mid-1800's. Elly chose rich, strong colors, including deep reds, blues, greens and golds that are typical of Baltimore Album Quilts and that are true to that era.

With Heart and Hand

Elly contributed this quilt label for use on any of the projects in this book or for any other project that deserves a beautiful final touch. You can use the "card" space to add the quilt title, quiltmaker's name, recipient or any other information.

Please note that fabrics are identified with P&B codes for the Baltimore Beauties III (BBE3) collection.

Yardage and Supplies

Background: #860G (green) = Cut one piece 9 1/4" x 12"

Frame: #866B (blue) = Cut one piece 6 3/4" x 9 1/4"

Oval: #866Y (yellow) = Scrap at least 6" x 8"

Hand: #861R (red/orange) = Scrap at least 4" x 6"

Card: #866P (pink) = Scrap at least 3" x 4"

Small scraps of the following:
  Sleeve: #861B (blue)
  Cuff: #861Y (yellow)
  Heart: #866R (red)

Paper-backed fusible web = 1/3 yard

Perle cotton or embroidery floss

Embroidery or chenille needle

Optional:
  Fine point (.01) permanent fabric marker
  Applique press sheet

NOTE: All appliqué templates are shown as finished sizes. Add seam allowance as needed, depending on your appliqué method. For your convenience, templates have already been reversed (where necessary) to allow you to trace directly onto your paper-backed fusible web. This will allow your finished label to look the same as the sample.

Construction

Trace templates onto the paper side of the fusible web following manufacturer's instructions. Iron web onto the back of fabric and cut out pieces directly on the drawn lines. Add any writing to the card while the paper is still in place on the web, as this will help to stabilize the fabric as you write.

Remove paper backing from the web. Begin by placing frame onto the background and press. Add the following in order: oval, card, hand, sleeve and cuff. Add heart. *TIP: Using an appliqué press sheet will help you to arrange all the pieces as they should be before pressing onto the background. This eliminates multiple exposures to the heat of the iron, which may lift the design.*

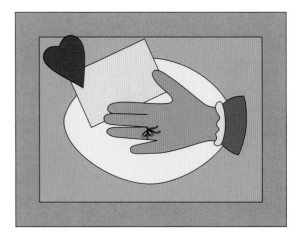

Placement of elements

Use matching perle cotton or embroidery floss to embroider buttonhole stitches around all raw edges. This could also be done on the sewing machine with 40 wt. or 50 wt. thread if your machine has the appropriate stitch. You might want to vary the size of the stitch depending on the size of the appliqué shape.

Take a stitch and wrap a piece of embroidery thread around the ring finger of the hand. Tie it with a bow and tack it down with more of the same thread. Applique this quilt label to the back of your quilt, use it as a block within a quilt, or back, quilt and bind it using your favorite method.

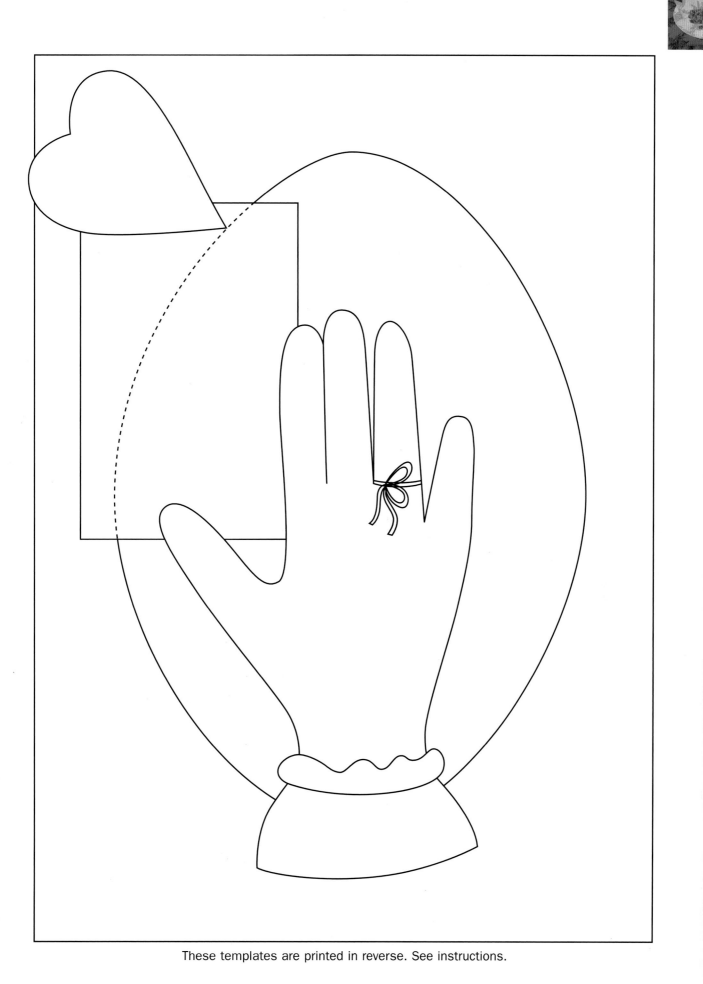

These templates are printed in reverse. See instructions.

Home and Garden Wall Quilt

"I'm very fortunate that breast cancer has not touched my immediate family, but saddened to say that I know of others whom it has affected. I'm glad to be part of this joint effort in helping to further research to find a cure for breast cancer. It would be wonderful if this disease could be wiped out entirely."

By Julee Prose ◆ Utilizing the *Baltimore Beauties III* collection ◆ Finished size: 44" x 44"

Julee Prose is a native of Ottumwa, Iowa, and she has been quilting since 1974, when she learned the basics from her grandmother. She is largely self-taught and works mostly in a very traditional style. In the early 1980's she owned a mail order quilting business, Kalico Keepsakes, for which she designed quilt patterns, wall quilts and quilting hoops for wall hangings.

Julee's quilts have won many awards in Iowa. She also won a first place award at the 1987 AQS show in the theme category. That quilt now hangs at the AQS Museum. She is currently a member of the Ottumwa Quilt Guild and has previously organized quilt clubs and chaired local quilt shows. She has been married for almost thirty years and has one son and two grandchildren.

Home and Garden Wall Quilt

Please note that fabrics are identified with P&B codes for the Baltimore Beauties III (BBE3) collection.

Yardage and Supplies

Center background: #860E (light tan) = ²⁄₃ yard

Inner border and binding: #867R (floral) = ³⁄₄ yard

Outer border: #865E (tan) = 1 ³⁄₈ yards

Vines: #860G (green) = 1 yard

Assorted leaves: #861G and #864G = ¹⁄₈ yard each (can also use some of #860G-all are green)

Roof, house trim and vases: #862B (dark blue) = ¹⁄₃ yard

Fat quarter or less of the following:

Rabbit: #864Z (light brown)

Cat: #862Z (brown)

Door: #863B (light yellow)

Windows: #860Y (yellow)

Window sashes: #864C (purple)

Tulip centers: #861B (light blue)

House and decorations on vases: #861Z (taupe)

Tulips: #866B (blue)

Flowers and buds: 4-10 different reds, pinks and yellows

Backing: 1¹⁄₂ yards of your choice of P&B 90" backing, or piece the backing from 3 yards of 45" fabric.

Fine point (.01) permanent fabric marker or embroidery floss

NOTE: All appliqué templates are shown as finished size. Add seam allowance as needed, depending on your appliqué method. All strips are cut selvage to selvage unless otherwise noted.

Cutting

Center background: #860E (light tan) = Cut (1) 24" square.

Inner border and binding: #867R (floral) = Cut (4) 2" strips. Trim (2) to 21¹⁄₂" and (2) to 24¹⁄₂." Reserve remaining fabric for binding.

Outer border: #865E (tan) = Cut (4) 10¹⁄₂" strips *lengthwise.*

Construction

CENTER BLOCK: Lightly mark the vine onto the background fabric, using the line drawing as a guide. Using your favorite method, prepare *finished* ¹⁄₄" bias vines and stems for the heart-shaped center vines. Applique the vines in place, leaving openings to insert the stems.

To construct the house, lightly mark the window and door frames onto the house fabric. Cut, prepare and appliqué the window and door frames onto the house fabric. Repeat with the window and the door. Use a permanent fabric marker or embroidery to add the windowpane lines and the doorknob. Applique the house on top of the vine. Cut, prepare and appliqué the house trim. Repeat for the roof, leaving openings to insert the chimneys.

Add the stems and buds to the vine. Cut, prepare and appliqué the roses to the vine. To begin, first sew a small center to a larger center and then add this unit to the rose. Sew the roses to the vine.

TIP: If you wish to reduce bulk within the roses, trim away the excess layers after sewing.

Complete the center square by sewing the leaves, rabbit and cat to the background. Add details to the faces of the animals with permanent fabric marker or embroidery. Center the design and trim the background fabric to measure 21¹⁄₂" square.

INNER BORDERS: Sew a 21½" border strip to each side of the center square. Press seams away from middle. Sew a 24½" strip to the top and bottom and repeat pressing.

OUTER BORDERS: Cut and sew the borders to the center square, stopping at the *seam point* on each end of every border to allow for mitering corners. Press seams away from the middle. Complete the miters and press those seams flat. Following the line drawing and the photo on page 12, lightly mark the vines onto the borders, using the seams and the center of each border as guides.

Note that the vines are sewn to the borders as four separate pieces. Cut, prepare and sew the vines and stems as for the center block, noting that the borders require ½" bias. Add the stems and leaves. Layer the tulip centers behind the tulips and sew them on. Sew the hearts and teardrops onto the vases and then appliqué them to the corners. Sew the centers onto the roses and then appliqué the roses on the mitered corners.

Layer quilt top, batting and backing. Quilt around all of the appliqué pieces. Add quilting on top of the pieces where there is more than one layer of appliqué, such as roses, tulips, vases and windows. Quilt gridwork in the background on the center square and on the outer border. Finish with binding, using reserved fabric #867R (floral).

Quilt Construction

Roof

Chimney

Baltimore Beauties III

"I am particularly pleased to have been included in this book because of its focus on raising both awareness of and funds for further breast cancer research."

By Julie Sheckman ◆ Utilizing the *Baltimore Beauties III* collection ◆ Finished size: 46" x 46"

Julie

*Julie Sheckman grew up in Chicago and later attended the
University of Miami in Florida, where she studied photography.
She has been a quilter for almost twenty years and has been
involved in numerous design and commission projects for several
textile manufacturers. Julie has a grown daughter, Jennifer, and presently
lives with her husband, Larry, in Blue Bell, PA, outside of Philadelphia.*

Baltimore Beauties III

Please note that fabrics are identified with P&B codes for the Baltimore Beauties III (BBE3) collection.

This project is constructed as raw-edged applique with optional straight stitch machine embellishment around each edge. The easiest way to accomplish this is to outline stitch each appliqué before adding the next one. You may want to slightly lengthen the stitch. The color of the thread is noted after each appliqué instruction.

Yardage and Supplies

Block background: #860Y (yellow) = ¾ yard
Center teardrop appliqués: #866R (red) = ¼ yard
Circle appliqués, dots and binding: #861O
 (red/orange) = 1 yard
Corner appliqués: #861Y (yellow) = ⅜ yard
Lattice and inner borders: #861G (green) = ½ yard
Small center square appliqué: #862R (dark red) =
 2" x 10"
Block and outer borders: #868R (floral) = 1½ yards
Backing: 1½ yards of your choice of P&B 90"
 backing or piece a backing.

2 yards Steam-A-Seam 2

Optional:
Mettler Cordonnet thread for outline stitching
 (use on top of machine only). Thread colors:
 #830 (tan) and #601 (burgundy).
Size 90 or 100 machine needle to accommodate
 thread

NOTE: All appliqué templates are shown as finished size. Add seam allowance as needed, depending on your appliqué method. All strips and segments are cut selvage to selvage unless otherwise noted.

Cutting

Block background: #860Y (yellow) =
 Cut (9) 8½" squares.
Circle appliqués, dots and binding: #861O
 (red/orange) = Cut off a 14" fabric segment to use
 for circles and dots and follow instructions below.
 Set aside remaining fabric to use for binding.
Lattice and inner borders: #861G (green) =
 Cut (8) 1½" strips. Take (2) of these strips and
 cut them into a total of (6) 12½" pieces. Take
 (4) more of these strips and trim them to 38½"
 pieces. Trim the final (2) to 40½" pieces.
Block and outer borders: #868R (floral) =
 Following Diagram A, begin by cutting (4) 3½"
 lengthwise strips for outer borders. Trim (2)
 strips to 40½" and (2) strips to 46½". Use
 remaining fabric to cut (15) 2½" strips across
 the *width*. Cut (6) of these strips into a total of
 (18) 8½" pieces. Cut the remaining (9) strips
 into a total of (18) 12½" pieces.

Diagram A: Cut lengthwise strips first

Construction

BLOCKS: Finished block size: 12." There are (9) blocks in this quilt. For each block, sew (1) 8½" strip of block border fabric to each side of background square. Press seams away from center. Sew (1) 12½" strip to the top and bottom to complete basic block. Repeat pressing.

Following product instructions, apply Steam-A-Seam 2 to the back of the following fabrics: #866R (red), #861Y (yellow), #862R (dark red) and the remaining piece of #861O (red/orange).

From prepared #861O (red/orange), use Template A on page 25 to trace (9) 6" rings onto paper side of product. Cut out the rings and save centers to use for smaller circles. Center and fuse a circle to each block. Embellish both edges with an outline stitch, using thread color #601 (burgundy).

TIP: To help center the circle, fold both the block and the circle in quarters and pinch folds to mark creases. Unfold both and align the crease marks.

From prepared #861Y (yellow), cut (9) 1" strips. Cut these into (72) 5" pieces. Following Diagram B, cut one end of each piece at a 45 degree angle. Note that half of the pieces are angled in one direction and the other half are angled in the opposite direction. Following Diagram C, place one of these pieces with the long side 5" in from the raw edge of one corner of the block. Place another piece in the same way, being careful to match and miter the angled edges. Fuse into place. Repeat for remaining (3) corners. Embellish with thread #830 (tan). Repeat for all blocks.

Diagram B1: Make 36

Diagram B2: Make 36

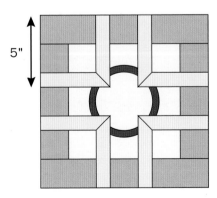

5"

Diagram C: Block construction and element placement

From prepared #866R (red), use template (page 25) to cut (4) teardrop shapes for each block. Fuse into place using drawing and photo on page 20 as a guide. Embellish with thread #830 (tan).

From prepared #862R (dark red), cut (9) 1" squares and fuse one on point to the center of each block. Embellish with thread #601 (burgundy).

LATTICE AND INNER BORDERS: Using fabric #861G (green), sew (1) 12½" strip vertically between the sides of the blocks creating (3) rows of (3) blocks each. Press seams toward lattice. Sew (1) 38½" strip between each row and also to the top and bottom. Repeat pressing. Sew (1) 40½" strip to each side and repeat pressing.

OUTER BORDERS: Using fabric #868R (floral), sew (1) 40½" strip to both sides of quilt. Press toward borders. Sew (1) 46½" strip to top and bottom of quilt. Repeat pressing.

Use the reserved 5" circles of #861O (red/orange) and cut (52) ¾" circles. You can use Template A or trace a penny.

Fuse into place, referring to schematic and photo for placement. Embellish with thread #601 (burgundy).

Layer quilt top with batting and backing. Quilt as desired. The sample quilt shows stippling, but avoids the appliqué pieces.

Bind using reserved fabric #861O (red/orange).

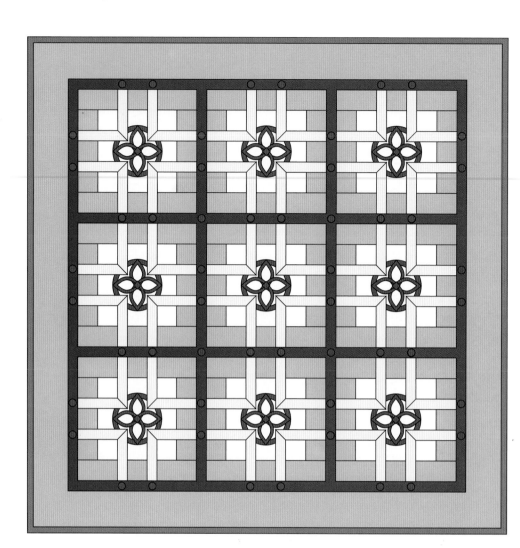

Quilt Construction

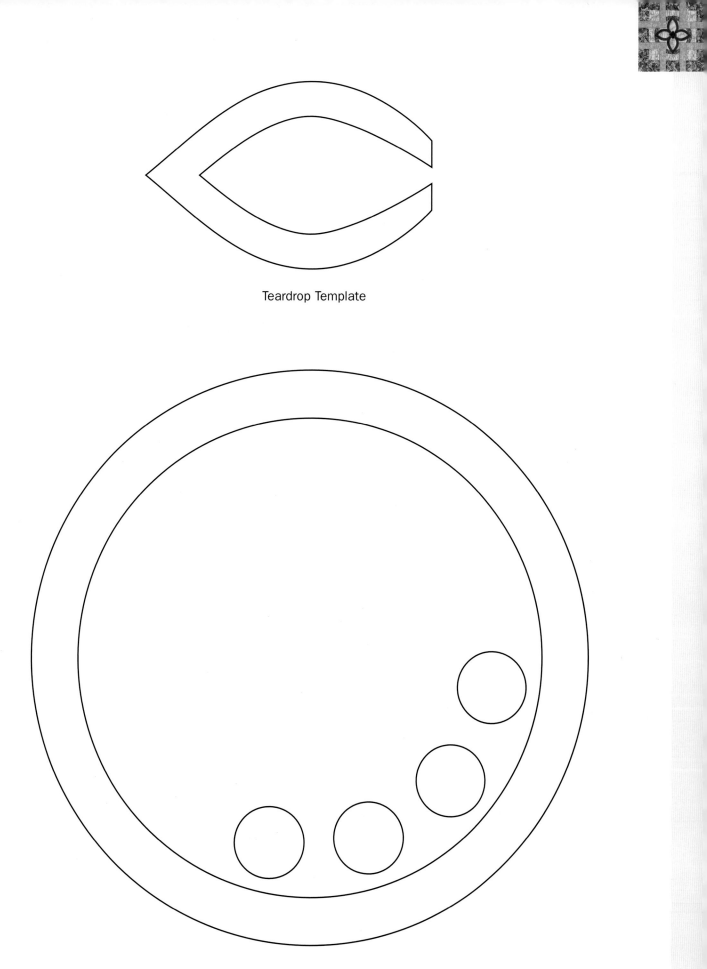

Teardrop Template

Template A

Tribute to Marian

"Most, if not all, have been touched by the sorrows of cancer and the triumphs of surviving cancer. The triumphs are better. This book has been a blessed opportunity to give something of myself that can eventually contribute to a cure."

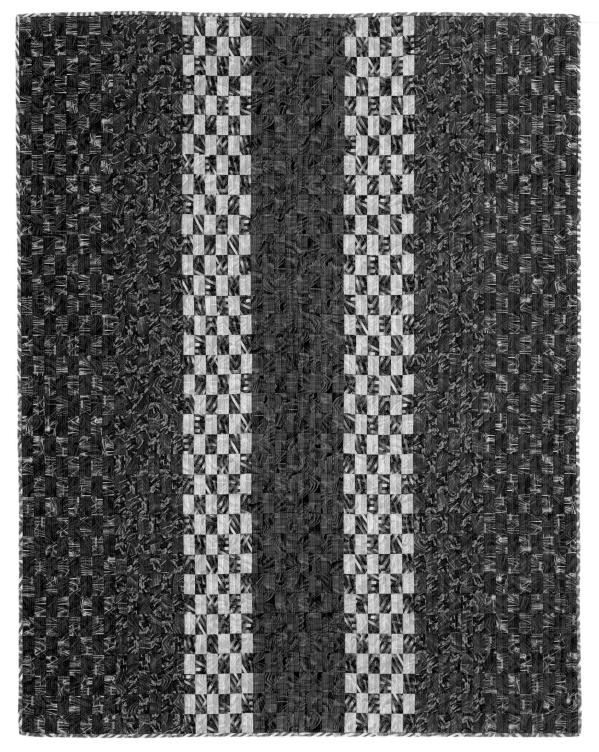

By Andrea Balosky ◆ Utilizing the *Century of Progress* collection ◆ Finished size: 60" x 72"

Andrea Balosky has been quilting for more than thirty years. She continues to be intrigued by the rhythm, as well as the orchestration, of simple, repeated shapes. These keep her absorbed and happy. Andrea teaches, lectures and writes about quilting. Her work has been exhibited regionally, nationally and internationally. A native of Hawaii, she now lives in central Oregon.

CENTURY OF PROGRESS COLLECTION
from the Allentown Art Museum

These Art Deco reproductions were inspired by a group of 1920's and 30's silk dress fabrics, which were designed to illustrate the contemporary culture of America. The Museum collection includes 2,500 selections of fabric, each documented with a date and record of the designer. All were originally purchased at New York department stores and later donated to the Museum. The fabrics chosen for this quilt include strong, architectural geometrics created by industrial designer Walter Dorwin Teague and inspired by the science and technology theme at the 1933 Chicago Exposition.

Tribute to Marian

"Marian Vieira Leong, my sister-in-law, is a recent breast cancer survivor. This quilt affirms my love and respect for her."

Please note that fabrics are identified with P&B codes for the Century of Progress (ALLE) collection.

Yardage

Blue panels: #239N (blue) and #237N (navy) = 1 yard each

Red panels: #239R (red) and #236R (orange) = ¾ yard each

Green panels: #239A (avocado) and #235G (green) = ¾ yard each

Purple panel: #239D (maroon) and #238C (purple) = ½ yard each

Backing: 4 yards of your choice of 45" wide fabric

Binding: #235S (gray) = ½ yard

NOTE: All strips and segments are cut selvage to selvage unless otherwise noted.

Cutting

For panels, cut all panel fabrics into 1¾" strips.
For blue panels, cut (18) strips of each color.
For red and green panels, cut (14) strips of each color.
For purple panel, cut (9) strips of each color.

Construction

The quilt consists of seven vertical panels. All panels are assembled by strip piecing.

From each color grouping, sew all the strips into pairs, one strip of each color. Sew pairs together, alternating the two colors, to create strip sets containing the following number of strips:

Blue: (8) alternating strips
Red: (6) alternating strips
Green: (6) alternating strips
Purple: (8) alternating strips

TIP: *Sew all initial pairs together in one direction. Then sew the pairs to other pairs, starting from the opposite end to avoid warping and to keep the strip set flat.*

Press seams in one direction (toward the darker color) throughout each grouping. (*NOTE: Be sure to do final press from the right side to avoid pleats within seams.*) Cut across the strip sets in 2½" segments (Diagram A). Blue, red and green sets require (72) of these segments. Purple set requires (36).

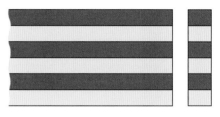

Diagram A: Basic strip sets

Position segments in alternate directions to achieve a rectangular checkerboard effect (Diagram B). Sew them together carefully, matching intersections and raw edges at beginning and end of seam. Previous pressing will provide the necessary opposing seams for convenient sewing. Sew (36) segments together for each color panel. Press all seams in one direction.

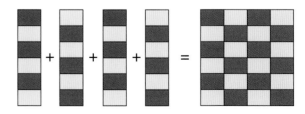

Diagram B: Creating the checkerboard

Following the schematic and photo, sew the panels together in order from left to right: blue, red, green, purple, green, red, blue. Flipping the panels in alternate directions will create opposing seam directions.

Layer, baste and quilt. The sample has a hand-quilted straight line running vertically through the center of each row. The thread color matches the panel colors.

Bind using your favorite method.

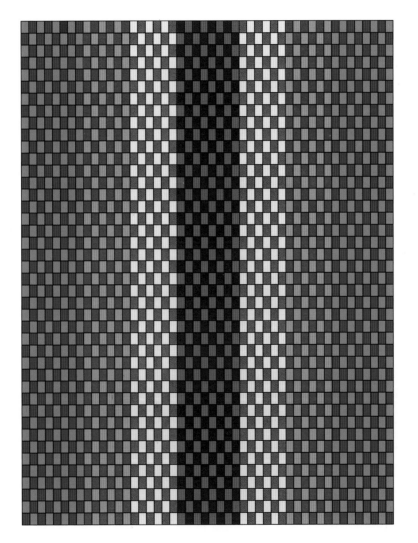

Quilt Construction

Bridge of Life

"This project spoke to me for the health and future of my daughter and her children yet to be born."

By Alex Anderson ◆ Utilizing the *Color Bridge* collection ◆ Finished size: 66" x 72"

Alex

Alex made her first quilt in 1978 as part of her art degree from San Francisco State University. Her emphasis on fiber and graphic design gave her a deep respect and admiration for Amish quilts. She has focused on understanding fabric relationships and surface design.

Alex currently hosts Simply Quilts *on* Home and Garden *television and has written numerous popular books on all aspects of quilting. She also has a monthly column in* Quilter's Newsletter Magazine, *and she still finds time to stay at home and quilt.*

THE COLOR BRIDGE COLLECTION
by Alex Anderson

Alex's idea behind *Color Bridge* was to create monochromatic prints with many hues that would help blend together many varying fabrics from the same color family. Because her red fabric, for instance, contains a variety of reds, it helps bring together disparate red fabrics, so they work with each other. Alex was frustrated that many of the older fabrics in her stash would not work with the newer ones, and her solution was manifested in this brilliant, color-filled collection.

Bridge of Life

Please note that fabrics are identified with P&B codes for the Color Bridge (CBRI) collection.

This quilt uses P&B Color Spectrum N (white) for the background as well as all (41) fabrics in the Color Bridge collection.

Yardage and Supplies

Background, backing and binding:
   Color Spectrum W (white) = 8 ¾ yards

Colored squares, baskets, flowers and leaves:
   (41) Color Bridge fabrics = ¼ yard each

Green vine and stems:
   your choice of green Color Bridge fabric = 1 yard

Optional
   ~ ³⁄₈" bias bar for the vines and stems
   ~ Embroidery floss in a variety of colors to complement the baskets
   ~ Short piece of pink ribbon

NOTE: All strips and segments are cut selvage to selvage unless otherwise noted. All appliqué templates are shown as finished size. Add seam allowance as needed, depending on your appliqué method.

Cutting

White background:

Basket blocks: Cut (6) 5" strips. Cut these into (42) 5" squares.

Nine Patch blocks: Cut (12) 2" strips. Cut these into (224) 2" squares. Save the remainder of the twelfth strip for the pieced border.

Setting triangles: Cut (2) 7 ⁵⁄₈" strips. Cut these into (7) 7 ⁵⁄₈" squares. Cut these squares diagonally in both directions. Only (26) of these quarter-square triangles are needed.

Corner triangles: Cut (2) 4" squares and cut both in half diagonally to produce (4) half-square triangles.

Pieced borders: Cut (10) 3 ³⁄₈" strips. Cut these into (106) 3 ³⁄₈" squares. Cut these squares diagonally in both directions to produce (424) quarter-square triangles. Cut the remaining 2" strip into (16) 2" squares. Cut these in half diagonally to produce (32) half-square triangles.

Appliqued borders: Cut (4) 6 ⁷⁄₈" strips from the lengthwise grain (parallel to the selvage). Save the remaining fabric to use for binding.

Color Bridge fabrics:

Nine Patch blocks and pieced borders: Cut (1) 2" strip from each of the (41) fabrics and cut each into at least (12) 2" squares. There will be a few extra squares to play with when arranging the fabrics within the pieced borders.

Appliques: Using templates, cut (42) baskets, (36) flowers, (36) flower centers and (24) leaves. *NOTE: Alex used green for leaves, and yellow and orange for flower centers. She used red, blue, purple and pink for flowers.*

Vine and stems: Cut approximately 300" total of 1 ¼" wide bias strips.

Construction

NINE PATCH BLOCKS: Referring to quilt photo and Diagram A, arrange and sew together (5) 2" Color Bridge squares and (4) 2" white squares. Press seams toward Color Bridge fabrics. Make a total of (56) blocks.

Diagram A: Nine-patch block – Make 56

BASKET BLOCKS: Prepare the appliqué baskets following your preferred method of appliqué. Center the baskets diagonally on the 5" white background squares so the block will finish on-point (Diagram B). Stitch the baskets to the squares. Alex chose to use embroidery floss to hand stitch a buttonhole stitch around each basket. Press the blocks from the back, preferably on a padded surface. Make 42 basket blocks.

Diagram B: Basket block on point – Make 42

PIECED BORDERS: Referring to Diagram C, sew the short side of one white quarter-square triangle to opposite sides of a Color Bridge square. Create (204) sets that are shaped like a parallelogram. Press seams as indicated by the arrows in the diagram. These are Unit 1.

Diagram C: Unit 1 – Make 204

Now create (16) corner units for the borders using quarter- and half-square triangles (Diagrams D and E). Note that (8) are left-side units, which are Unit 2, and (8) are right-side units, which are Unit 3. Press seams as indicated.

Diagram D: Unit 2 – Make 8

Diagram E: Unit 3 – Make 8

For each Inner Side Pieced Border, sew (22) sets of Unit 1 together with a Unit 2 at one end and a Unit 3 at the other end. Sew the units so that the points of the squares touch each other (refer to photo). Press.

For the Inner Top and Bottom Pieced Borders, sew (21) sets of Unit 1 together with a Unit 2 at one end and a Unit 3 at the other end. Press.

For each Outer Side Pieced Border, sew (30) sets of Unit 1 together with a Unit 2 at one end and a Unit 3 at the other end. Press.

For the Outer Top and Bottom Pieced Borders, sew (29) sets of Unit 1 together with a Unit 2 at one end and a Unit 3 at the other end. Press.

QUILT ASSEMBLY: Arrange the Nine Patch blocks, Basket blocks, setting and corner triangles in a diagonal set. Make sure you are pleased with the layout before you begin sewing. Sew into rows. Press seams away from the Nine Patch blocks. Sew the rows together, matching corners, and press seams in one direction.

Sew the Inner Side Pieced Borders to the quilt and press seams toward the center of the quilt. Sew the Inner Top and Bottom Pieced Borders to the quilt top and press seams toward the center of the quilt.

Your quilt should now measure 49 3/8" x 55 3/4". Trim (2) of the 6 7/8" white border strips to 55 3/4". Sew to the sides of the quilt. Press seams toward this border. Trim the remaining (2) 6 7/8" strips to 62 1/8". Sew to the top and bottom of the quilt. Press seams toward this border.

Sew the Outer Side Pieced Borders to the quilt top. Press seams toward the wide border. Sew the Outer Top and Bottom Pieced Borders to the quilt top. Press seams toward the wide borders.

APPLIQUED BORDERS: Prepare one continuous bias tube finished at 3/8" wide for the vines and stems using your preferred method. Cut (4) vines 50" long and (24) stems 2 1/2" long. Prepare the (36) flowers and flower centers and (24) leaves following your preferred method of appliqué. Stitch the flower centers to the flowers. Position the vine, stems, flowers and leaves onto the borders. Use the photo and the schematic to help with placement. Stitch all elements to the border. Press from the back, preferably on a padded surface.

Layer, baste and quilt as preferred. The quilt sample has diagonal cross-hatch quilting within the block area of the quilt and the outer pieced border. The stitching continues directly through the baskets in the blocks. The appliqué borders are ditch-quilted around the flowers, centers, leaves and vines. In addition, there is a cable/feather design quilted around the appliqué areas.

Bind using your favorite method. Label your quilt.

OPTIONAL FINISHING TOUCH: Alex tacked a pink ribbon loop onto one of the basket blocks located near the center of the quilt.

Quilt Construction

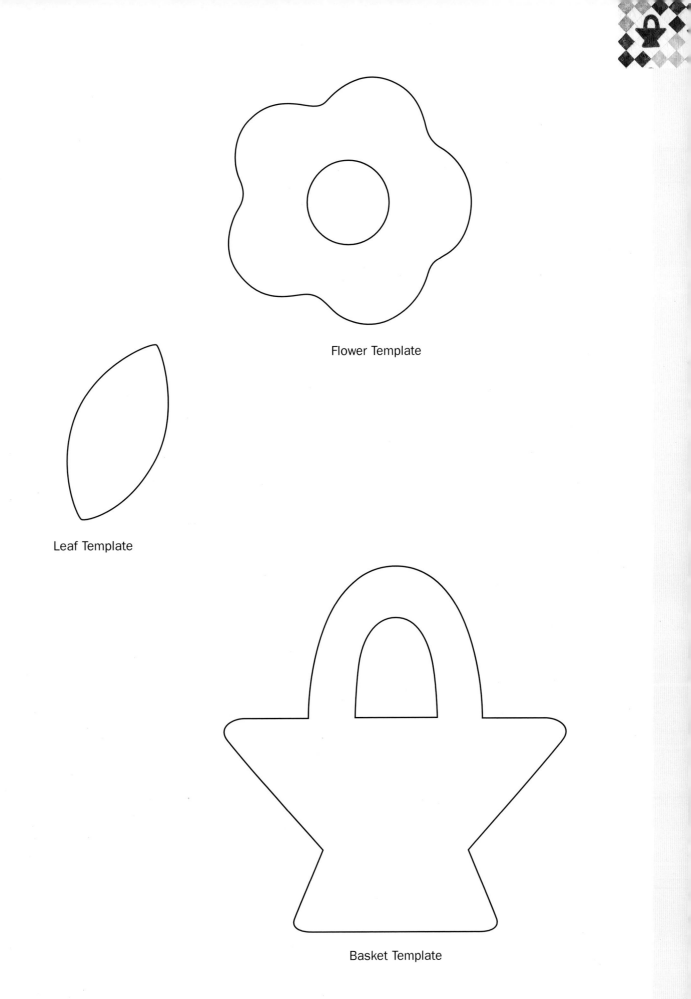

Flower Template

Leaf Template

Basket Template

Color Bridge Dance

By Alex Anderson ◆ Utilizing the *Color Bridge* collection ◆ Finished size: 42" x 42"

Color Bridge Dance

"This quilt celebrates the day I received one-yard cuts of my first fabric collection, *Color Bridge*. There are eight different patterns covering the colors of the rainbow, forty-one pieces in all. *Color Bridge* fabrics are monochromatic prints that have several color variations within one color family. These fabrics were created to ease the transition of using many variations of one color family within a quilt. As I enjoyed each piece and the subtle color differences, I stroked, petted and tactilely connected with each piece. Then it was time to cut! Off of each piece came a 3⅞" strip. I then lined them up in color sequence. It was interesting how well the colors played with each other (not the original intention of this fabric line). As the colors delighted my eyes, I decided to let them play together, thus inspiring the fabric's 'first dance!' Feel free to try out your own style of dance with this fabric collection. Let your creative spirit soar with *Color Bridge*!"

Yardage

⅓ yard cuts of all 41 fabrics in the collection
Backing: 1¼ yards

Cutting and Piecing

This quilt is made up of (288) 3" finished half-square triangles. There are (44) 6" finished quarter-square triangles and (4) 6" half-square triangles in the border.

For the center of the quilt, cut (5) or (6) squares of each fabric at 3⅞" and then cut them in half diagonally. Arrange them on a fleece wall according to the picture. You may need to cut a few more half-square triangles of certain colors (Alex put an orange star in one corner). Once you have an arrangement that is pleasing to your eyes, sew the triangles into square units. Join the squares into rows, and then join the rows together, being careful to match seam points and corners.

The borders are made up of (44) quarter-square triangles. Decide on the fabrics that you want to use and cut them into (11) 7¼" squares. Cut them diagonally in both directions, like an "X". **(TIP: The red acts as a neutral and pulls the other colors together in perfect harmony.)** Arrange the colors in a pleasing manner.

For the corners, cut (2) 6⅞" squares and cut in half diagonally.

Once you are pleased with the arrangement of the border triangles, sew the quarter-square triangles together first. First add these borders to the top and bottom of the quilt and then add the side borders. Press seams toward borders. Finally, sew the corner triangles to complete the quilt top and press toward the triangles.

Layer, baste and quilt. The quilt shows large-scale wavy quilting meandering throughout the block area with the exception of the orange star in the corner. The star is ditch-quilted. The outer border uses large-scale zigzag quilting, which flows into the outer row of block triangles. Free-form stars are quilted in the outer inverted triangles.

Note that the binding is pieced from a variety of blues, teals and purples.

Quilt Construction

Tennessee Garden

"I am happy to donate a quilt to this project because breast cancer touches almost everyone, both friends and relatives. It was nice to be asked to participate."

By Mabeth Oxenreider ♦ Utilizing the *Garden Plan* collection ♦ Finished size: 59 ½" x 76 ½"

Mabeth

Mabeth Oxenreider has enjoyed quilting for more than twenty years and has been teaching for eighteen of those years. She loves getting students excited about the quilting process. Mabeth has had many quilts juried into major shows, winning several top prizes. She says the process of taking a great original design and applying color and good techniques gives her a very heartwarming and humbling feeling.

Liz

Liz Lauter is the designer of the Garden Plan *fabric* collection from which this quilt was created by Mabeth Oxenreider. Liz is an independent designer and artist whose love and knowledge of botany and gardening heavily influence her designs. She completed her B.A. in Fine Arts at UC Davis and studied extensively with then-faculty member, Wayne Thiebaud. For a decade she ran a wearable art gift company exclusively featuring her designs. Liz currently teaches high school photography, ceramics, and art in Larkspur, California.

THE GARDEN PLAN COLLECTION
by Liz Lauter

Liz Lauter has strong backgrounds in both botany and fine art, which led to this enchanting collection. She created whimsical garden vignettes that include plants and animals, fountains and statuary, grass, flowers and a rambling brick pathway. The group includes a diminutive toile based on scenes from the other prints. Liz has combined a delicious array of colors to create a most memorable garden display.

Tennessee Garden

Please note that fabrics are identified with P&B codes for the Garden Plan (GPLA) collection, except where noted.

Yardage and Supplies

Centers of garden blocks: #446YG (panel print) = 1½ sets (8 panel squares)

Centers of garden blocks: #440G (vignette print) = 1 yard

Center of star blocks, second border and pieced border: #447YG (floral) = 1½ yards

Star block and pieced border: #442O (bricks) = 1½ yards

Four-patch: #443B (blue floral) = ½ yard

Four-patch: #445B, E, P, L (toile) = ¼ yard each

Star blocks, first border, pieced border and binding: Skywriting Collection SWRI #171N (blue swirl) = 2 yards

Backing: your choice of Garden Plan fabric = 4 yards

Template plastic

NOTE: All strips and segments are cut from the width of fabric unless otherwise noted. Templates include seam allowances.

Cutting and Piecing

There are (18) pieced 9" star blocks and (17) 9" alternate garden blocks.

PIECED STAR BLOCK: Cut (3) 3½" strips of #442O (bricks) and use Template A to cut (72) triangles, placing the template alternately across the strip, as in Diagram A. Cut (5) 3½" strips of SWRI #171N (blue swirl). Use Template B to cut (72) triangles and use the reverse of Template B to cut (72) triangles, as in Diagram B. Sew one B triangle and one B-reverse triangle to either long side of an A triangle to create a square that contains two star points, as in Diagram C. Sew (72) sets.

Diagram A: Template A placement

Diagram B1: Use Template B to cut 72 triangles

Diagram B2: Use reverse of Template B to cut 72 triangles

Diagram C: Make 72 sets

Cut (8) 2" strips of #443B (blue floral). Cut (2) 2" strips from each toile fabric. Sew one toile strip to a #443B (blue floral) strip and press seams toward the #443B (blue floral) fabric. Cut the strips into 2" segments, as in Diagram D. Arrange (2) of these pieces into a four-patch unit that contains two floral squares and two different toile squares, as in Diagram E. Sew a total of (72) four-patch units.

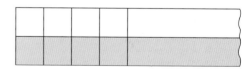

Diagram D: Cut sewn strips into 2" segments

Diagram E: Make 72 four-patch units

Cut (2) 3 ½" strips of #447YG (floral) and then cut them into (18) 3 ½" squares. Use these as the center squares of the star blocks. Following Diagram F and photo, sew (18) star blocks.

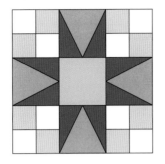

Diagram F: Sew 18 star blocks

GARDEN BLOCK: "Fussy cut" (8) 9 ½" squares from #446YG (panel print) and (9) 9 ½" squares from #440G (vignette print).

TIP: *Cutting a 9 ½" square of template plastic can be helpful when centering motifs within the design area.*

Cut (6) 3 ½" strips of #442O (bricks), then cut into (68) 3 ½" squares. With right sides together, place one square over each corner of each garden block. Referring to Diagram G, sew diagonally across each small square.

Diagram G1: Sew diagonal seams

TIP: *You may find it easier to draw or fold a diagonal line across the squares first.*

Trim away the extra fabric leaving a ¼" seam allowance. Press these seams toward the triangles. Sew (17) garden blocks.

Diagram G2: Sew 17 blocks

Following schematic and photo, lay out the blocks, alternating the star blocks with the garden blocks. When you are pleased with the arrangement, sew blocks into rows and join rows together, matching corners.

BORDERS: For the first border, cut (6) 1 ¾" strips of SWRI #171N (blue swirl). Join these together and then cut this piece into (2) 45 ½" lengths and (2) 66" lengths. Sew top and bottom borders and then sides. Press all seams toward the borders. For the second border, cut (3) 1 ¼" strips of #447YG (floral). Join together and from this piece cut (2) 48" lengths for the top and bottom. Cut (3) 2 ¼" strips of #447YG (floral). *NOTE: The side borders are slightly wider.* Join together and from this piece cut (2) 68 ½" lengths for the sides. Add these strips to the quilt in the same manner.

PIECED BORDERS: Cut (6) 2" strips from #171N (blue swirl) and #442O (bricks). Use the same method as described in the star block directions to create (60) four-patch units from these two fabrics. Cut (4) 5 ½" strips of #447YG (floral) and then cut into (28) 5 ½" squares. Cut each square diagonally twice to produce (112) quarter-square triangles. Cut (8) 3" squares of the same fabric and cut each in half diagonally to produce (16) half-square triangles.

Following schematic and photo on page 38, sew the short side of two of the quarter-square triangles to opposite sides of a four-patch unit, as in Diagram H (see Diagram H and note [*] on next page). Create (52) sets that are shaped like a parallelogram (there are (8) remaining four-patch units).

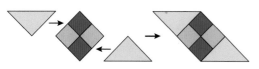

Diagram H: Create 52 sets

Diagram J: Create 4 of each unit

Sew (10) of the sets together for both the top and bottom borders as in Diagram I. Sew (16) sets together for the side borders.

Diagram I: Sew 16 sets

TIP: *The blue squares will create a line, all touching point to point, for the long sets. The orange squares will create the same line for the short sets.*

Follow Diagram J to create (8) corner units for the borders. Note that (4) face in one direction and (4) face in the opposite direction.

Add the appropriate unit onto each end of the longer border pieces to create squared ends. You should now have two borders with (12) four-patch units and two borders with (18) four-patch units and corner units. Sew the shorter borders to the top and bottom of the quilt and then sew the longer borders to the sides.

Layer, baste and quilt. The quilt has diagonal quilting stitched in both directions through all blocks. In addition, there is a "spider web" quilting design in the garden blocks. All other quilting is done in-the-ditch.

Bind with #171N (blue swirl), using your favorite method.

Note the positions of the orange and blue squares in the borders. The blue squares always point vertically in each four-patch.

Quilt Construction

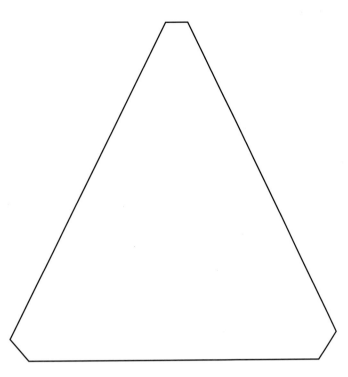

Template A

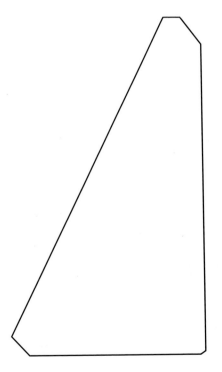

Template B

Woven Star

"I believe when we are offered the opportunity to give back to our community, we should jump at the chance to make a difference. Participating in this project has allowed me to do what I do best, so that others can do what they do best in medical research and education. Together we can make a difference."

By Karen Montgomery ◆ Utilizing the *Pine Garland I and II* collections
Finished size: 70" x 70"

Karen

Karen Montgomery is the owner of The Quilt Company in
Alison Park, PA, a store she opened in 1993. She has published
a line of books and patterns that are sold all over the world. She
teaches classes in her store, around the country and at International
Quilt Market. Karen has a degree in interior design from the Art
Institute of Pittsburgh. She has previously designed cross-stitch patterns
and has been a Regional Craft Coordinator for major craft stores. She is
married and has three children.

THE PINE GARLAND II COLLECTION
by Karen Montgomery

Karen has styled a wonderful holiday collection featuring a charming
blend of old-fashioned ornaments, pine boughs and swags, holly,
berries and pinecones. She mixes maroon, hunter green, gold and
tan to fashion a festive feast for the eyes. This group, combined
with her first *Pine Garland* collection, can span the season from
Thanksgiving to the end of the year.

Woven Star

Please note that fabrics are identified with P&B codes for the Pine Garland (PGAR) collections.

Yardage

Stars: #155W (stripe) = 1½ yards

Background for blocks: #153HG (dark green) = 1 yard

Light backgrounds, alternate star points and border: #153E (tan) = 1½ yards

Alternate star points: #153G (medium green) = ⅜ yard

Pieced border: #153W (off-white) = ½ yard

Pieced border: #156G (pine print) = 1¾ yards

Sashing and pieced border: #153R (red) = 1 yard

Cornerstones: #153D (dark red) = ¼ yard

Binding: #152G (green plaid) = 1 yard

Backing: 4¼ yards of 45" fabric or 2⅛ of 90" fabric

NOTE: All strips and segments are cut across the width of the fabric unless otherwise noted.

Cutting

Stripe for stars: Cut the 1½ yard piece of #155W (stripe) into two pieces, each measuring ¾ yard. Carefully cut from each of these pieces (8) 3½" strips on the *length* of the fabric. (Stripes will run parallel along the strips.) You will have a total of (16) strips. Vary the position of the stripe in each strip as much as possible to create variety within the stars, as in Diagram A. Cut each of these 3½" wide strips into (4) 6½" segments.

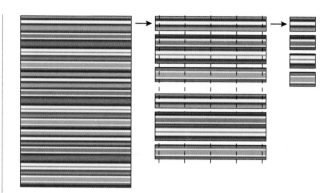

Diagram A: Cutting instructions

Dark green background for blocks: Cut (8) 3½" strips. Cut these into (96) 3½" squares.

Tan for light backgrounds, alternate star points and border: Cut (12) 3½" strips. Cut these into (144) 3½" squares. Cut (1) 4" strip and cut it into (8) 4" squares. Cut these in half diagonally once to produce (16) half-square triangles.

Medium green for alternate star points: Cut (3) 3½" strips. Cut these into (32) 3½" squares.

Off-white for pieced border: Cut (2) 3½" strips. Cut these into (16) 3½" squares. Cut (1) 4" strip and cut it into (8) 4" squares. Cut these in half diagonally once to produce (16) half-square triangles.

Pine print for pieced border: Cut (3) 3½" strips. Cut these into (32) 3½" squares. Cut (6) 4½" strips. Cut these into (16) 12½" rectangles. Cut (1) 7½" strip. Cut into (4) 7½" squares. Cut (3) 2" strips. Cut into (20) 6" rectangles. Cut (1) 4¼" strip. Cut into (8) 4¼" squares and cut these diagonally in both directions (X) to produce (32) quarter-square triangles.

Bright red for sashing and pieced border: Cut (14) 2" strips. Cut these into (40) 12½" rectangles. Using the leftover ends of these strips, cut (20) 2" squares. Cut (1) 2⅝" strip. Cut into (16) 2⅝" squares.

Dark red for cornerstones: Cut (2) 2" strips. Cut these into (25) 2" squares.

Construction

BLOCKS: Select half of your stripe segments to be used with the light background star blocks and the other half with the dark background star blocks. Working with the dark background first, arrange one set of four matching rectangles on your worktable. Check to be sure that each of the segments is positioned right side up and facing in the same direction. Using a pencil, chalk or permanent marker, draw a diagonal line on the wrong side of each of the 3½" dark green squares. Stitch, corner to corner, directly on the drawn line, as in Diagram B. Trim the excess fabric, leaving approximately ¼" seam allowance. Press. Make (8) sets. Repeat the steps with the remaining stripe segments, substituting the tan squares for the dark green squares.

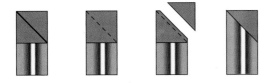

Diagram B: Creating a diagonal corner

TIP: For the next two steps of the block construction, match the background fabrics with the point square fabrics as follows: Background 153HG (dark green) with point square 153E (tan); and background 153E (tan) with point square 153G (medium green). Refer to photo as needed.

Create the alternate star points by placing a 3½" background square and a 3½" point square right sides together, as in Diagram C. Mark a diagonal line and stitch directly on the drawn line. Trim as before, leaving a ¼" seam allowance. You will need (32) dark green/tan sets and (32) medium green/tan sets.

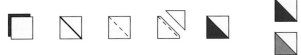

Diagram C: Make 32 dark green/tan units, and 32 medium green/tan units

Assemble the star blocks, as in Diagram D. Make (8) light background and (8) dark background blocks.

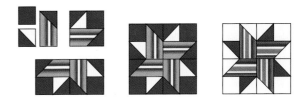

Diagram D: Make 8 dark blocks and 8 light blocks

CENTER OF QUILT: Arrange the completed star blocks in (4) rows of (4) blocks each. Alternate the dark and light background blocks. Assemble the center of the quilt top by adding the 2" x 12½" red sashing rectangles vertically between the blocks within each row. Add these sashing pieces at the beginning and end of these rows as well. Press seams toward the sashing. Create the long sashing sections that will be sewn horizontally between the rows. Sew these rows by alternating (4) sashing pieces with (5) dark red cornerstones. Begin and end each row with one of the cornerstones. Press these seams toward the sashing. Sew these sashing rows between the block rows, carefully matching the seams of the sashing and cornerstones. Press.

PIECED BORDER: Aligning the corners, stitch the short sides of the pine print quarter-square triangles to adjoining sides of the red 2⅝" squares, as in Diagram E. Press seams toward the triangles. Center and stitch an off-white half-square triangle on the bottom left of the completed unit. Press seam toward triangle. Repeat, using a tan half-square triangle on the right side of the unit. Trim and square this unit to measure 3½" x 6½". Make (16) units.

Diagram E: Make 16 units

Create the half-square triangle sets for either side of the previous unit. Use the 3 ½" squares of the pine print combined with the 3 ½" squares of both off-white and tan fabrics. Use the technique described in alternate star points (page 47). You will need (16) pine print/off-white and (16) pine print/tan sets. Stitch a completed set to either end of the center unit from above. Position the off-white set to the right of the center unit and the tan set to the left of the center unit, as in Diagram F.

Diagram F: Make 16 units

Stitch the (16) red 2" squares to one end of the (16) pine print 2" x 6" rectangles. Press seam toward the pine print. Assemble (4) identical border units, as in Diagram G.

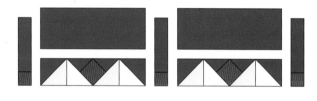

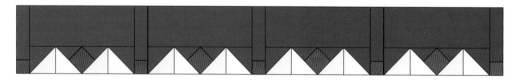

Diagram G: Assembly and finished unit – Make 4

Add a 7 ½" corner square to each end of two of the borders, as in Diagram H. Press toward the squares.

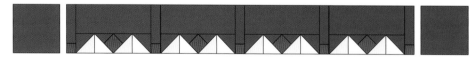

Diagram H: Make 2

Matching seam intersections, pin the shorter border units to the sides of the quilt. The bright red squares should align with the dark red corner-stones of the sashing strips. Sew and press toward quilt. Sew the remaining borders to the top and bottom of the quilt, matching seam intersections. Press.

Layer batting, backing and quilt top. Quilt as preferred. The sample quilt shows quilting in-the-ditch within the stars and lattice. Stippling is used in both the dark and light-colored background areas. The border contains horizontal channel quilting.

Bind using your favorite method.

Quilt Construction

Fancy Flowers

"I am delighted to support breast cancer research. They do a great job of educating women on the importance of early detection. Early detection has saved the lives of many of my friends and family members." Linda

"I have had three breast biopsies. I was ecstatic they were all negative. But before the test results came back, I was sure that I had breast cancer. In that short space of time I realized that I was not ready to die. I am happy to support breast cancer research, so that someday soon, when a woman gets a diagnosis of breast cancer, it is not so frightening." Becky

By Linda Jenkins and Becky Goldsmith, Piece O' Cake Designs
Utilizing the *Seasonings* and *Woven Stripes and Plaids* collections ◆ Finished size: 48 ½" x 48 ½"

Linda & Becky

Becky Goldsmith was born and raised in Oklahoma City, where she earned a degree in interior design at the University of Oklahoma. She has been quilting for fifteen years. She and her husband, Steve and their two boys live in Sherman, Texas.

Linda Jenkins is originally from Tulsa and just returned there. She worked for more than twenty years as a hair stylist and salon owner, and began quilting as a hobby in 1984. She loves all aspects of quilting, but her favorite is needleturn applique.

Linda and Becky started their quilting business, Piece O' Cake Designs, in 1994. They now travel and teach nationwide, have written seven books, published numerous patterns and Block of the Month collections, and have designed many award-winning quilts.

THE SEASONINGS and WOVEN STRIPES AND PLAIDS COLLECTIONS

by Piece O' Cake Designs

Seasonings is offered in four colorways to represent spring, summer, fall and winter. In *Seasonings*, Becky and Linda fashioned a superb collection of fruit, florals, stripes and snowflakes that combine elegance with a touch of whimsy, maintaining Becky and Linda's buoyant character while adding a sophisticated tone. They have also collaborated on an exciting collection of woven plaids and stripes to delight the eye.

Fancy Flowers

Please note that fabrics are identified with P&B codes for the Woven Plaids and Stripes (POCP) collection and the Seasonings (SEAS) collection.

Yardage and Supplies

Border and block background: POCP #105E (tan stripe) = 1 1/3 yard

Additional block backgrounds: POCP #104E (tan plaid) and SEAS #719E (tan print), #725E (tan dot), #727EE (tan stripe) – total of 1 1/4 yards
NOTE: You'll need a total of (16) 10" squares of background fabrics.

Border and sashing corners: POCP #107B = 1/4 yard

Border corners: SEAS #719E (tan print) = 1/4 yard

Sashing and applique: SEAS #719R (red print) = 1/2 yard

Additional applique fabrics: POCP #113R (red stripe), #106G (green stripe), #102B (blue check), New Basics #33Y (yellow) and New Basics Classics #15 (brown) = 1/3 yard each

Binding: POCP #113R (red stripe) = 3/4 yard

Backing and sleeve = 3 yards of POCP or SEAS Red embroidery thread

80 red buttons in three sizes (you can substitute with red fabric if you wish)

Cutting

Block background: Cut (16) 10" squares from a variety of fabrics.

Border background: Cut (4) 8" x 36" rectangles.

Border corners: Cut (8) 3 1/2" squares from each of the two fabrics. Fussy cut the plaid fabric to make sure the plaid is straight.

Sashing: Cut (12) 2" x 16 1/2" strips. Cut (8) 2" x 6 1/2" strips.

Sashing corners: Cut (9) 2" squares.

Binding: Make a 2 1/2" wide continuous bias strip from a 26" square.

NOTE: Applique patterns are drawn to finished size.

Construction

BLOCKS: Piece together (4) different 10" background blocks for each square. Make (4) squares. Use the seams as your guidelines for placement of each quarter-section of the block applique (see Diagram A). Rotate the guideline, and use the photo to determine placement of your applique pieces. Use your favorite applique method. Embroider the berry stems with two strands of cotton embroidery floss in a backstitch. If you are creating the "berries" in applique, add them now. If you use buttons instead, omit them for now. When you have completed the blocks (without the buttons), trim each of them to 16 1/2" square.

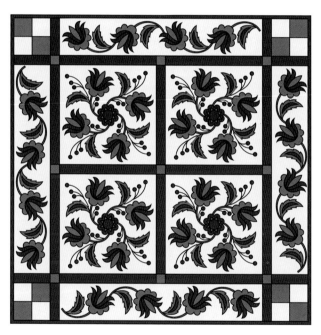

Quilt Construction

Vertical Center Seam Line

Horizontal Center Seam Line

Diagram A: Applique placement, one-quarter of each block

Finished Inner Edge of Border

Lengthwise Center of Border

Finished Outer Edge of Border

5

6

7

4

3

2

1

Diagram B: Pattern for border design

BORDERS: Using Diagrams B (page 54) and C as guides, arrange the flowers, leaves and stems on the border background pieces. The first and third flowers match Diagram B. Reverse the pattern for the second and fourth flowers. Note that the flower stem in Diagram B has two possible lengths. Use the shorter stem ending for flower #4. Make (4) border pieces. Trim borders to 6½" x 34" after the applique is complete.

Diagram C: Placement of elements in border pieces

Use the 3½" border corner squares to create (4) four-patch blocks. See Diagram D.

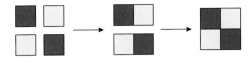

Diagram D: Create the four-patch blocks

Sew together the blocks, borders, corner squares, sashing and sashing blocks as shown in Diagram E.

Diagram E: Sew the quilt pieces together

Layer, baste and quilt. The sample quilt has stitching around all of the applique pieces and stipple quilting in the background. Add the button "berries," sewing through all layers.

Add binding, documentation patch and sleeve.

Healing Hearts

"An awareness of breast cancer, its proximity and frequency, is simply a fact of life for women today. In my life, this illness has touched the lives of an aunt, a cousin and several close friends. Being a part of this book allows me to add my voice to the many others who are emphasizing the need for a cure and the funding for research to achieve this goal."

By Nancy Taylor ♦ Utilizing the *Woven Stripes and Plaids* collection ♦ Finished size: 55" x 55"

Nancy

Nancy Taylor is a former co-owner of the quilt shop, Going To Pieces in Pleasanton, CA. A visually-oriented person, Nancy excels at drawing and visual expression. She studied at the University of Michigan's College of Art, and has worked as an illustrator at a large corporation and as an interior designer at an architectural firm. Fabric has always been a medium of expression for her, and her quilts include commercially printed fabrics as well as her own designs, created by dyeing, painting, stamping, spraying and screen printing fabrics. Nancy currently works full time on her textile collages and quilts.

Healing Hearts

Please note that fabrics are identified with P&B codes for the Woven Plaids and Stripes (POCP) collection and the other collections used.

Nancy has combined four P&B collections to make this quilt. Although each block has a different combination of fabrics, each includes one component made from the Woven Plaids and Stripes collection. Nancy used machine satin stitch combined with fusible web to complete the appliquéd hands.

Yardage and Supplies

Hands, background squares and squares for 2nd and 3rd pieced borders: POCP #106G (green plaid) , 111R (red plaid), 103B (blue stripe), 102B (blue plaid), 101A (avocado stripe), 100A (avocado plaid), 112Y (yellow stripe), 110P (pink plaid), 108B (blue/green plaid), 107B (multi plaid), 113R (red stripe), 109R (red/yellow plaid) = $1/3$ yard each

Triangles for second pieced border: POCP #104E (tan plaid) and 105E (tan stripe) = $3/8$ yard each

Background squares, hands, hearts and first pieced border: = $1/3$ yard each

  New Galaxy collection NATG #165B (blue), 165C (purple), 165K (black), 165F (fuschia), 165R (red), 165LB (light blue)

  Shadows collection SHAD #182F (fuschia), 182R (red), 182C (purple)

  Skywriting collection SWRI #170R (red), 170L (lavender), 170Y (yellow), 170B (blue), 170LB (light blue), 170G (green)

Binding: SHAD #182C (purple) = 1 yard

Backing: $3 1/2$ yards (45" width) *or* $1 3/4$ yards (90" width) *or* piece a variety of leftover fabrics

Optional: 1 yard lightweight fusible web

NOTE: All appliqué templates are shown finished size. Add seam allowance as needed, depending on your appliqué method. All strips and segments are cut selvage to selvage unless otherwise noted.

Cutting

NOTE: The plaids are oriented diagonally within the triangles of the second and third borders. To achieve this effect, the triangles are cut resulting in bias edges for both of these borders. Please be aware and treat these sections carefully to avoid any stretching of the fabric.

BACKGROUND SQUARES FOR BLOCKS: Cut (16) $9 1/2$" squares from a variety of fabrics as described in Yardage and Supplies.

HANDS AND HEARTS: Apply appropriate-sized pieces of fusible web to the wrong side of a variety of fabrics (unless you are using traditional applique methods). Trace the template onto the paper side of web and cut out on drawn line. You will need (16) hands and (16) hearts. For variety, reverse the template on some hands.

FIRST PIECED BORDER: Cut a total of (16) rectangles $9 1/2$" x $1 3/4$" plus (4) $1 3/4$" squares. Use a variety of the New Galaxy, Shadows and Skywriting collections.

SECOND PIECED BORDER: Cut (40) $3 1/2$" squares from a variety of the Woven Plaids and Stripes collection. Cut (22) $3 7/8$" squares from each of POCP #104E (tan plaid) and #105E (tan stripe). Cut each in half diagonally once to produce (88) half-square triangles.

THIRD PIECED BORDER: Cut (26) 7" squares from a variety of Woven Plaids and Stripes collection. Cut each in half diagonally to produce (52) half-square triangles. Cut (4) additional $4 3/4$" squares for the corners.

TIP: Before you begin cutting the squares, lay out your quilt and study it carefully. Note that the sample shows every other square in the second border touching a triangle of the same fabric in the third border (this isn't true for the corners). If you want this effect for your quilt, you will need to lay out all of your triangles before you sew them together. You can also choose to sew the fabrics together randomly and disregard Nancy's arrangement.

Construction

BLOCKS: Play with the placement and fabric combinations of the hearts and hands on the background squares. Try placing the hand in different directions and overlapping the heart in various places. When you are satisfied with the combinations, fuse the hearts and hands in place and machine appliqué them to the background squares. If you are using traditional appliqué methods, pin and stitch.

TIP: You may want to decide on all (16) blocks before you begin sewing any of them.

Once you have completed all the blocks, arrange them into a 4 x 4 pattern. Make sure that you are pleased with the layout and then sew the blocks together, matching corners. Press seams.

FIRST BORDER: Place the border rectangles (9½" x 1¾") into a pleasing arrangement around the outside of the blocks, remembering to include the small corner squares. Sew the side sets together. Press. Sew them to the sides of the center blocks, matching corners. Press away from center. Sew the top and bottom sets together, including the corner squares at the beginning and end of each set. Press. Sew to the top and bottom of center blocks. Press away from center.

SECOND BORDER: Sew the short side of a tan triangle to opposite sides of a plaid square to create a parallelogram shape, as in Diagram A. Press toward squares.

Diagram A

Begin sewing parallelogram sets together with points of the squares touching each other (refer to photo); sew two border side sections that each include (7) of these sets. The seams will be facing in opposite directions, enabling you to nest these seams, which will help the points of the squares to match each other.

You will need to construct corner units for both ends of these border sections. Following Diagram B, sew the short side of one triangle to a square in the same manner as the rest of the border. Sew the long side of two additional triangles to this unit to square off the ends. These triangles will be too large and should be trimmed and squared after they are pressed. You will be creating (4) left units and (4) right units.

Diagram B1: Left unit – Make 4

Diagram B2: Right unit – Make 4

Sew one of these units to each end of the side borders. Sew borders to sides of center. Press. Repeat this process to make two more borders each containing (9) parallelogram sets. Add triangles to the ends to square them, and then add to the top and bottom of the center.

THIRD BORDER: Sew (4) sets of (13) triangles together, creating a long border for each side, as in Diagram C (next page). If you plan to match plaids to the second border (as mentioned previously), you may want to lay out each border before sewing them. These borders will be too long at this stage.

Diagram C: Third Border

Pin two of the borders to the sides of quilt, starting from the center triangle and working out to the edges, matching points with the second border. Sew borders, then press carefully toward these borders. Trim off the excess fabric at the ends and square borders to quilt. Sew the remaining borders to the top and bottom of the quilt, leaving several inches unsewn at each end. Carefully measure the ends of the borders to match your quilt, including

the second border only. Add ¼". Add the corner squares to these ends and then sew the final seams to finish adding the borders to the quilt.

Layer batting, backing and quilt top. The sample uses echo quilting around the hearts and hands, with ditch quilting around the blocks and borders. Diagonal quilting lines were used through the two outer borders.

Bind using your favorite method.

Quilt Construction

Heart and Hand Templates

Window on the Tropics *(Retina Fatigue)*

"I have a firm belief that those of us who are lucky to be 'cursed' with this drive to create and to touch fabric will live longer, fuller lives. Being able to pass my drawings from my hands to yours through fabric and then through quilts extends my life and yours beyond our years. I dedicate this quilt to Sue Ackley in hopes that through the 'laying on of hands' our lives together will extend beyond this moment."

By Susie M. Robbins   ◆   Utilizing the *Tropical Fling* collection   ◆   Finished size: 69" x 77"

Susie

Susie M. Robbins was born and raised in Columbus, Ohio. She graduated from Miami University in Oxford, Ohio, and her design credits are from Ohio State University, the Cleveland Art Institute and Rhode Island School of Design. She minored in fabric design. Susie's company, Peddlers of Danville, *was formed when she started designing cloth dolls. Her quilt life began with Diana McClun at Empty Spools in Alamo, California, but it was not until 1989 that she actually designed her first commercial piece of fabric. Susie is driven by color and design and loves it. She says, "It is not often you get to play all day long and call it work. We all should be so lucky!"*

THE TROPICAL FLING COLLECTION
by Susie M. Robbins

Glorious orchids, hibiscus, clematis and other tropical flowers all abound in a profusion of beauty and color in this vibrant collection. The group includes a lush tropical foliage print with a very large repeat, a delicate clover-like oxalis pattern and an extremely unique fern jungle stripe. The colors are electrifying and vital — with detailed contour drawings rendered by Susie, based on Hawaiian flora. It's almost like taking a tropical vacation!

Window on the Tropics (Retina Fatigue)

Please note that fabrics are identified with P&B codes for the Tropical Fling (TFLI) collection.

"This quilt was designed to represent large windows that look into a tropical scene. The fabric contains patterns that are full of movement and colors that are quite intense. If you look at them for a period of time, your eyes may become tired! You may even feel dizzy! This feeling is called retina fatigue. However, most people will simply feel as though they've had a brief visit to Maui! Love the color, love the design and, above all, love the complete experience. Sew for the Cure®!"

Yardage and Supplies

Sashing, outer borders and binding:
  Color Spectrum #W (white) = 4 yards
Black background center of windows:
  #771K (orchid/black) = ⅔ yard
White background center of windows:
  #771W (orchid/white) = ⅔ yard
Black for first window frame:
  Color Spectrum #K (black) = ½ yard
Purple for second window frame, pieced sashing
  and stars: #774C (purple stripe) = ½ yard
Light green for second window frame, pieced
  sashing and stars: #774HG (olive stripe) = ½ yard
Yellow for third window frame, pieced sashing
  and stars: #770G (green jungle) = 1 yard
Purple for third window frame, pieced sashing
  and stars: #770C (purple jungle) = 1 yard
Red for stars and pieced sashing: #772R (red
  hibiscus) = ½ yard
Yellow for stars and pieced sashing:
  #772Y (yellow hibiscus) = ½ yard
Red/orange for stars, cornerstones and pieced
  sashing: #772O (orange hibiscus) = 1 yard

Backing: White or any Tropical Fling = 4 ½ yards
  45" wide fabric
Optional:
  Template plastic
  Flannel wall

NOTE: All strips and segments are cut selvage to selvage unless otherwise noted. Since templates include seam allowance, trace them exactly as shown.

Cutting

ORCHID WINDOWS: Using clear template plastic, prepare a template measuring 7 ½" x 10 ½". By placing this over the orchid fabrics, you will be able to center areas of the fabric within the "window." When you have experimented with different placement options, trace and cut (6) windows from the #771K (orchid/black) and (6) from the #771W (orchid/white). These windows will be placed alternately within the quilt.

FIRST WINDOW FRAME: Cut (12) 1" strips from solid black fabric. Cut each strip into (2) 7 ½" and (2) 10 ½" segments. Cut (2) 1" strips from #772O (orange hibiscus) and cut into (48) 1" squares.

SECOND WINDOW FRAME: Cut (6) 1 ½" strips from each of the #774C (purple stripe) and #774HG (olive stripe). Cut each strip into (2) 8 ½" and (2) 11 ½" segments. Cut (2) 1 ½" strips from #772O (orange hibiscus) and cut into (48) 1 ½" squares.

THIRD WINDOW FRAME: Cut (7) 2 ½" strips from each of the #770G (green jungle) and #770C (purple jungle). Cut (3) strips of each fabric into (12) 10 ½" segments. Cut (4) strips of each fabric into (12) 13 ½" segments. Cut (3) 2 ½" strips from #772O (orange hibiscus) and cut into (48) 2 ½" squares.

SASHING: Cut (31) 1 1/2" strips from the white fabric. Cut these strips into (32) 14 1/2", (30) 17 1/2" and (36) 3 1/2" segments. Cut (3) 1 1/2" strips from each of the seven fabrics listed above to be used for pieced sashing.

STARS: Cut a 2 3/8" strip from each of the star fabrics listed previously. Cut each strip into (12) 3" segments. Cut these rectangles in half diagonally to produce (24) triangles (Diagram A). These are the star points.

Diagram A: Cut 6 of each to create 24 triangles.

In addition, cut several 3 1/2" squares from each of the same fabrics. These are the star centers. There are extras of each piece. You will be arranging these pieces on your flannel wall to decide where to use the variety of stars.

OUTER BORDER: Cut (7) 3 1/2" strips. Cut these strips into (8) 14 1/2" and (6) 17 1/2" segments. There will be extra strips after cutting segments. Use this extra to cut (4) 3 1/2" squares for corners of the quilt.

Construction

FIRST WINDOW FRAME: Sew one short black strip to both sides of each window. Press toward window. Sew one 1" square to each end of both long strips. Press toward the squares. Sew these long frames to the top and bottom of each window, matching corners. Press toward the window.

SECOND WINDOW FRAME: Sew one short purple strip to both sides of the white background window blocks. Repeat using the short green strips for the black background window blocks. Press toward the sashing. Sew one 1 1/2" square to each end of all long strips. Press toward the sashing. Sew these long frames to the top and bottom of their respective blocks, matching corners. Press toward the sashing.

THIRD WINDOW FRAME: Using the window blocks that are now framed in purple, sew one short yellow strip to both sides. Repeat with the blocks now framed in green, using the short purple strips. Press seams of all blocks toward the sashing. Sew one 2 1/2" square to each end of all long strips. Press toward the sashing. Sew these long frames to the top and bottom of their respective blocks, matching corners. Press toward the sashing.

PIECED SASHING: Arrange and join together one strip from each fabric into a strip panel. (TIP: *Alternating sewing directions as you add each strip will help to avoid warping and keep the panel flat.)* Press all seams in one direction, being extra careful to press from front to avoid any pleating within seams. You will make (3) strip panels.

Cut (28) 1 1/2" segments from each panel. For each of the side sashing units, join (2) of these panel segments for a total of (16) units. There will be (14) small squares in each of these units. For each of the top and bottom units, join segments together for a total of (15) units. Each unit needs (17) small squares. You will need to remove stitching and join some segments together to achieve this. You will also need (18) end sashing units. Each unit needs (3) small squares.

COMPLETE SASHING: Sew (16) short sashing units by joining one 14 1/2" white strip to each side of corresponding pieced sashing unit, as in Diagram B (next page). Sew (17) long sashing units by joining one 17 1/2" white strip to each side of corresponding pieced sashing unit. Sew (18) end sashing units by joining one 3 1/2" white strip to each side of a corresponding 3 1/2" pieced sashing unit. Press all seams toward white sashing strips.

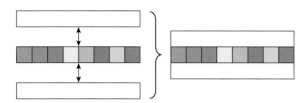

Diagram B: Sashing Unit

Use the arrow-shaped template on page 67 to trim both ends of each of the 14 1/2" and 17 1/2" sashing units, as in Diagram C. Trim only one end of each of the 3 1/2" units. To do this, place the point of the arrow even with the raw edge of fabric and centered within each end. Mark and then cut off the side corners, creating a pointed end.

Diagram C: Placement of template - Cut off corners

At this stage, you should arrange all parts of the quilt on a flannel wall or floor. Be sure to place the corresponding unsewn triangles and squares of the star fabrics together to complete the stars in the positions that you have chosen.

Once you have decided on an arrangement, finish sewing the sashing units. To do this, you will sew a set of star triangles to *each* end of the 14 1/2" and 17 1/2" sashing units, as in Diagram D. Sew a set of star triangles onto the pointed end of the 3 1/2" sashing units. Be sure to match corners of triangles to corners of sashing units. Note that the triangle seams cross below the typical 1/4" seam intersection. This is correct. Press all seams toward sashing.

Diagram D

To construct the four horizontal rows of the quilt, sew a 14 1/2" vertical sashing unit between each of the blocks, beginning and ending each row with a sashing unit (Diagram E). Press all seams toward blocks. Sew one 3 1/2" x 14 1/2" white outer border piece to each end of all rows. Press seams toward outer borders.

Now construct the five horizontal sashing rows that will be sewn between each of the block rows. Referring to the photo and Diagram E, sew the 3 1/2" sashing units, 3 1/2" star centers and 17 1/2" sashing units together. Press seams toward center star squares. Carefully matching seams, sew these sashing rows between the block rows, beginning and ending with a sashing row at the top and bottom of the quilt. Press seams toward blocks.

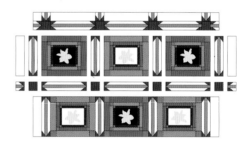

Diagram E: Main top construction

Construct the outer border units for top and bottom of quilt. Referring to photo on page 62 and diagram on page 67, sew the 3 1/2" white border squares, 3 1/2" sashing units and 17 1/2" sashing units together. Press seams toward the white border pieces. Sew to the quilt. Press seams toward blocks.

Layer, baste and quilt as desired. The sample quilting outlines some of the key motifs within the window of each block. Borders and stars were quilted in the ditch. The outer block border also contains a small continuous leaf design. The outer quilt border contains a larger continuous leaf design.

Bind using your favorite method. Don't forget to add a label!

Quilt Construction

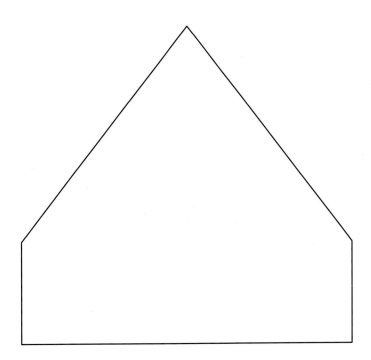

Somewhere in Paradise

"Breast cancer is the most prevalent form of cancer and has afflicted many friends and much-loved family members. In the name of all women who have suffered with this dreadful disease, it is a privilege and honor to be a part of a project that moves us closer to a cure for breast cancer." Kathleen

"Creative work lifts the spirits of the maker and the viewer. In the face of breast cancer, anything that can lift the spirit is important. If it can also help fund research for a cure, that much the better. I am not a scientist, so I have no hope of finding a cure, much as I wish I could. But I can design, so this is a way that doing something I love can help a scientist find a cure. A project like this is important because it raises awareness of the disease in a positive way that reaches people, unlike statistics and symptoms." Ann

By Kathleen Butts and Ann Marra ◆ Utilizing the *Tropical Fling* collection
Finished size: 48 ½" x 48 ½"

Kathleen

Kathleen Marra Butts began quilting in 1989, and it has been a full-time passion ever since. She has taught quilting classes in the Northwest, including hand quilting, hand applique, piecing and many of her own innovative techniques, such as construction of half-square triangles, double paper appliqué and multiple freezer paper piecing. She holds degrees in home economics and sociology, and she taught for more than twenty years in the Clothing & Textile departments at Iowa State University and Washington State University.

Ann

Ann Marra has owned her graphic design business since 1976. She specializes in high profile promotions for products and events, including everything from swim suits to conveyor belts. She learned to sew from her mother, Kathleen Butts, and made her first tailored suit at age sixteen. The advent of computers in the field of design left her with tactile deprivation, so she returned to quilting, and now collaborates with her mother on commissions for P&B Textiles. Ann recently relocated near her mother to continue developing the quilt design business, to breathe fresh air and to experience the joys of telecommuting.

Somewhere in Paradise

Please note that fabrics are identified with P&B codes for the Tropical Fling (TFLI) as well as other P&B collections. The fabrics are TFLI unless otherwise noted.

Yardage

Focus squares within blocks:
#771B (orchid/blue), 771K (orchid/black), 772C (purple hibiscus), 772O (orange hibiscus), 772P (pink hibiscus), 772R (red hibiscus), 772Y (yellow hibiscus), 773B (blue clematis), 773R (red clematis) = 1/6 yard or fat eighth

Fabrics used within the purple log cabin blocks:
#774C (purple stripe), 775C (purple oxalis), 773C (purple clematis), 770C (purple jungle) = 1/8 yard each ♦ Skywriting collection: #170B (blue), 171L (lavender), 172C (purple) = 1/8 yard each ♦ New Basics 2000 collection: #33RV (violet) = 1/8 yard ♦ Naturescapes collection: #165D (maroon) = 1/8 yard

Fabrics used within the green log cabin blocks:
#774G (green stripe), 775HG (olive stripe) = 1/8 yard each ♦ Skywriting collection: #170H (hunter), 170G (green) = 1/8 yard each ♦ Color Bridge collection: #934G (green) = 1/8 yard ♦ New Basics 2000 collection: #30YG (light green), 33G (green), 31YG (blue green), 32YG (yellow green) = 1/8 yard each

Sashing: #770O (orange stripe) = 1/2 yard

Green border corner squares: #774HG (olive stripe) = 1/4 yard

Purple border rectangles: #770C (purple jungle) = 1 yard

Binding: Skywriting collection #170B (blue wave) = 1/2 yard

Backing: 3 yards 45" wide fabric *or* 1 1/2 yards 90" wide fabric

NOTE: All strips and segments are cut from selvage to selvage unless otherwise noted.

Cutting

FOCUS SQUARES WITHIN PURPLE BLOCKS:
Each fabric lists the number of 4" squares needed from each one: #771K (1); 772C (2); 772P (2); 772R (2); 772Y (1).

FOCUS SQUARES WITHIN GREEN BLOCKS:
Each fabric lists the number of 4" squares needed from each one: #771B (2); 772O (2); 773B (2); 773R (2).

LOG STRIPS FOR PURPLE LOG CABIN BLOCKS:
(all strips are 1 3/4" wide)
#774C = Cut (1) strip; cut into (8) 4" segments.
#170B = Cut (1) strip; cut into (8) 5 1/4" segments.
#775C = Cut (1) strip; cut into (8) 5 1/4" segments.
#773C = Cut (2) strips; cut into (8) 6 1/2" segments.
#770C = Cut (2) strips; cut into (8) 6 1/2" segments.
#33RV = Cut (1) strip; cut into (5) 7 3/4" segments.
#172C = Cut (1) strip; cut into (1) 7 3/4" segment.
#165D = Cut (1) strip; cut into (2) 7 3/4" segments.

LOG STRIPS FOR GREEN LOG CABIN BLOCKS:
(all strips are 1 3/4" wide)
#934G = Cut (1) strip; cut into (2) 4" segments.
#170G = Cut (1) strip; cut into (3) 4" segments.
#31YG = Cut (1) strip; cut into (2) 4" segments.
#32YG = Cut (1) strip; cut into (1) 4" segment.
#774C = Cut (1) strip; cut into (8) 5 1/4" segments.
#775HG = Cut (1) strip; cut into (8) 5 1/4" segments.
#30YG = Cut (2) strips; cut into (8) 6 1/2" segments.
#33G = Cut (2) strips; cut into (8) 6 1/2" segments.
#170H = Cut (2) strips; cut into (8) 7 3/4" segments.

SASHING: Cut (11) 1 1/2" strips from #770O. Cut these into (52) 7 3/4" segments.

SASHING SQUARES: Cut (1) 1 1/2" strip from #934G. Cut into (25) 1 1/2" squares.

BORDER SQUARES: Cut (1) 7 3/4" strip. Cut into (4) 7 3/4" squares.

BORDER RECTANGLES: Cut (4) 7 3/4" strips. Cut into (8) 16" segments.

Construction

LOG CABIN BLOCKS: Follow Diagrams A and B, showing fabric and log placement within each block. Blocks are constructed in an off-center style, with log strips added to only two sides of the focus square. Start with the focus square, and add the shortest strip to one side. Press all seams away from focus square. Add the next shortest strip to the adjacent side of the square, overlapping onto the end of the first strip. Add the next shortest length to the same side as the first strip, again overlapping onto the previous strip. Continue in this fashion until the block is completed, with one focus square and six added strips (three each on two sides). Make 8 purple blocks and 8 green blocks.

Diagram A: Green log cabin

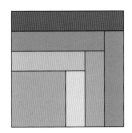

Diagram B: Purple log cabin

SASHING: Use photo on page 68 and drawing on this page to arrange blocks (note the placement of the focus square in each block). You will be sewing blocks first into horizontal rows. Working with one row of blocks at a time, sew one vertical piece of sashing between each block, beginning and ending the row with sashing. Press seams toward sashing. Repeat for remaining rows.

You will now need to sew (5) rows of horizontal sashing. Sew a sashing square between each piece of sashing, beginning and ending the row with a sashing square. Press seams toward squares. Matching seams carefully, sew sashing rows between block rows, beginning and ending with a sashing row. Press seams toward sashing.

BORDERS: Sew (4) border sections that consist of sashing, border rectangle, sashing, border rectangle and sashing. Press seams toward border rectangles. Sew one of these sections to each side of quilt. Press seams toward borders. Sew one border square to each end of the remaining border sections. Press seams toward sashing. Sew one of these border sections to the top and the bottom of the quilt. Press seams toward borders.

Layer, baste and quilt as preferred. The sample quilt has quilting in-the-ditch within the log cabin blocks. There is also outline quilting around some of the key motifs within the block centers, as well as in the outer border and corners.

Bind using your favorite method. Label your quilt.

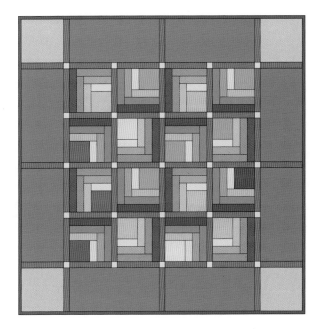

Quilt Construction

Recipes

THE RECIPE COLLECTION

It's probably common knowledge that quilters love to eat. After
all, both cooking and quilting are art forms and comfort activities,
so it makes sense that people often, though not always, enjoy both
pursuits. We've asked the quilters involved in this book, along
with several P&B staff members, to contribute their favorite
recipes for your enjoyment. Some are more complicated, and
some are quick and easy (to give you more time for your quilting!).
We offer the recipes grouped according to courses. Dessert seems
to be the favorite, of course!

RED SALSA

From Becky Goldsmith

"This is my husband Steve's recipe. I don't actually cook, so you don't want one from me!"

2 16-oz. cans diced tomatoes
1 8-oz. can tomato sauce

1 can chopped green chiles
1 medium onion, finely chopped
Fresh or pickled jalapeños or serranos, to taste (usually 2 or 3 is enough for jalapeños; 4 or 5 for serranos; I also use the carrots and onions in the pickled jars)
¼ C white vinegar
½ of a lime – squeeze juice, then finely chop the peel and add it, too
1 tsp. garlic powder, or 2-3 cloves fresh garlic, pressed
Chopped cilantro (optional)

Use blender or potato masher to puree the canned tomatoes. Pour into a medium saucepan and heat. Chop the onion and peppers and add to the tomatoes and sauce. Add the green chiles, vinegar and lime. Simmer until the onions are tender. After it cools some, add the garlic. Add some chopped cilantro if you like. Serve warm or cool.

Appetizers

CRABCAKE MUFFINS

From Karen Montgomery

6 English muffins
5-7 oz. can of crabmeat
¾ stick margarine
5 oz. jar Kraft Old English Cheese
½ tsp. garlic salt
1 Tbs. minced onion
1½ Tbs. mayonnaise
¼ tsp. pepper
Paprika

Slice English muffins in half and set aside. Soften margarine and cheese. Mix these together with the remaining ingredients and spread onto English muffin halves. Place on cookie sheet and bake at 350 degrees for 15-20 minutes. Cut each muffin into quarters and sprinkle with paprika. Serve warm.

These muffins can be stored in the freezer, unbaked, for up to three months.

Soup

BROCCOLI/CAULIFLOWER SOUP FOR THE SOUL

From Elly Sienkiewicz

2 C chicken or turkey broth, skimmed of fat

1 quart broccoli cut into thumb-sized chunks

1 quart cauliflower cut into similar chunks

$^1\!/_2$ C butter

1 C finely minced onion

3 tsp. curry powder

6 C whole milk

$4^1\!/_2$ Tbs. cornstarch

1 Tbs. oregano

1 C packed fresh parsley, finely chopped

2 lemons, cleanly sliced into $^1\!/_4$" rounds

NOTE: To save time, use two 10-ounce packages each of frozen chopped broccoli and cauliflower and dried or frozen minced onions. To save calories, use skim milk.

Steam broccoli and cauliflower in a pot with the broth. Leave the lid cracked open $^1\!/_2$" to keep the green broccoli bright. Steam until al dente. When slightly cooled, puree half a quart at a time until not quite smooth.

Melt the butter in the bottom of a gallon-size soup pot. Blend in the curry. Add the onion and sauté these together until onion is clear but crisp. Blend in the milk and cornstarch and bring the mix to a boil. Add the vegetable puree. Add oregano, then salt and pepper to taste. Serve topped with parsley and lemon slice as a garnish. Suggest to your guests that they press the lemon against the bowl with their spoon to release the juice.

Makes 12 cups.

Salads

SOUTHEAST ASIA SALAD

From Andrea Balosky

1 small head Napa cabbage, thinly sliced
1 bunch watercress, stemmed
1 large handful spinach, sliced
2-3 C bean sprouts
$1/2$ small red onion, thinly sliced
$1/4$ C skinned, shelled peanuts, toasted in pan and crushed
Small handful each of basil, cilantro and fresh mint
3 cloves garlic, sliced
2 Tbs. canola oil
2 Tbs. fresh lime juice
2 Tbs. soy sauce
2 tsp. honey
$1/4$ tsp. chili flakes

Mix cabbage, watercress, spinach, bean sprouts and onion in a bowl. Heat oil in saucepan and fry garlic until brown and crispy. Remove from heat and add lime juice, soy sauce, honey and chili flakes. Stir, cool slightly and pour over salad. Sprinkle herbs and peanuts on top.

Salads

SPINACH SALAD

From Kathleen Butts

2 lbs. cauliflower, chopped into bite-sized pieces
1 lb. fresh spinach, cut into 1/2" strips
3/4 C olive oil
6 Tbs. white wine vinegar
2 large cloves garlic, pressed
1 tsp. salt
1 tsp. dry mustard
1 tsp. basil
1/2 tsp. freshly ground pepper
1/8 tsp. freshly ground nutmeg
2 C toasted slivered almonds
2 avocados, sliced
lemon juice
4 slices bacon, cooked crisp and crumbled

Wash and prepare cauliflower and spinach. Make dressing from oil, vinegar, garlic and spices. Toast almonds. When ready to serve, slice avocados and coat with lemon juice. Toss spinach and cauliflower with salad dressing. Add almonds and avocados and toss lightly. Garnish with bacon crumbles.

Serves 12.

Salads

RAMEN NOODLE COLESLAW

From Julee Prose

2 pkg. Ramen creamy noodle soup (dry)
$\frac{1}{2}$ C sugar
$\frac{1}{3}$ C cider vinegar
$\frac{1}{4}$ C olive oil
16 oz. coleslaw
$\frac{1}{2}$ C slivered almonds (optional)

Mix 2 seasoning packets from the soup with the sugar, vinegar and oil. Mix in coleslaw. Keep chilled. When ready to serve, crumble dry noodles into mix and stir. Sprinkle with almond slivers.

Variation: Add a can of mandarin orange slices or pineapple tidbits.

Salads

SPICY PASTA SALAD

From Nancy Taylor

For the Dressing:
¼ C white vinegar
¼ C seasoned rice wine vinegar
4 Tbs. freshly squeezed lime juice
4 Tbs. sugar
4 tsp. toasted sesame oil
2 cloves garlic, minced
1 tsp. red pepper flakes

For the Salad:
½ lb. vermicelli
2 carrots, grated
1 large red bell pepper, chopped
2 C mushrooms, sliced
1 bunch cilantro, stems removed, chopped
1 C dry roasted peanuts, chopped

Combine dressing ingredients in a lidded container. Shake until sugar is dissolved and ingredients are blended.

Break pasta into thirds and cook until al dente. Rinse and drain well.

In a large bowl, combine pasta and dressing, mixing well. Add the carrots, red pepper, mushrooms and cilantro, and combine thoroughly. Top with chopped peanuts.

SHRIMP AND FETA CHEESE PASTA

From Alex Anderson

"This is SOOO good and easy to make. This recipe will generously feed two hungry folks."

1 lb. extra large raw shrimp (remove from shell and devein)
1-2 Tbs. butter
Juice from 1 lemon
2 cloves garlic, chopped
4 green onions, sliced into $1/8$" pieces
4 oz. feta, cut into small cubes
4 Tbs. capers
1 lb. penne pasta

While the pasta is cooking, melt the butter with the lemon in a frying pan and brown the garlic. Right before the pasta is cooked, toss in the shrimp, onions and feta. One minute before the shrimp is cooked, add the capers. Serve over the cooked pasta.

PESTO CORSINI

From Deborah Corsini

"In the summer, basil is abundant at the Farmer's Markets. I make this recipe often and freeze half for a delicious taste all year around."

1 bunch (4 C) basil, tightly packed
⅓ C olive oil
½ C toasted pine nuts
6 cloves garlic

Remove stems from basil. Wash and spin dry leaves to remove all water. In the food processor, finely chop the garlic cloves. Add the basil and chop until very fine. Add the pine nuts and olive oil and blend. Makes enough pesto for 10-12 servings.

To Serve:
Cook pasta of choice – spaghetti or linguini are excellent. In a frying pan, heat the pesto (approximately 1-1½ tsp. per person). Add 2-3 tsp. water from the cooking pasta and stir to a smooth consistency. Drain the pasta and mix with the pesto in the frying pan. Add salt and pepper to taste.

Optional:
Any of the following may be added to the final dish for color and taste: whole toasted pine nuts, Parmesan cheese, cherry tomatoes, roasted red peppers.

KILLER BROWNIES

From Ann Bear

1 lb. caramels
¼ C caramel ice cream topping or caramel sauce
¾ C butter or margarine, melted
⅔ C evaporated milk
1 pkg. (18.5 oz.) Swiss or German chocolate cake mix
1 C chopped nuts, optional
1 C semisweet chocolate chips

On top of double boiler, over medium heat, combine caramels and ⅓ C evaporated milk, stirring until smooth. While you are doing that, preheat oven to 350 degrees and grease a 9" x 13" pan.

Combine cake mix, melted butter and ⅓ C evaporated milk in mixer until well blended. Spread half of cake mix into pan and bake 6 minutes. Once the caramels are smooth, remove from heat, then add ¼ C caramel topping (or sauce) to the melted caramels and mix together. Take out cooked portion of brownies when done and sprinkle chips and nuts evenly over crust. Pour remaining caramel mixture evenly over chips/nuts. Dollop remaining cake mixture over caramel. Return to oven and bake another 15-18 minutes (it will still be gooey when done). Cut into SMALL squares (it's sweet!). *Hint: If you place them face down on a tray when serving, they may not look as nice, but they stick less!*

Dessert

PINEAPPLE BREAD PUDDING

From Julie Sheckman

"This recipe has been handed down from friend to friend to friend. It's great with the savory part of the meal or as dessert with ice cream."

1½ C sugar
1 C butter, soft
3 eggs, beaten
20 oz. pineapple, crushed
6 C day-old bread (about 8 slices), cubed

Cream together the sugar and butter. Add the beaten eggs and pineapple. Combine with the cubed bread and pour into a 13" x 9" pan. Bake at 350 degrees for about an hour or until golden brown.

Dessert

G'MA'S APPLE TART

From Crystal Streeter

1 cube butter, melted, plus 1 Tbs. hard
1 C flour plus 1 Tbs.
2 Tbs. vinegar
¼ tsp. salt
3 Pippin apples, cut up
½ C sugar plus 1 Tbs.
1 tsp. cinnamon

Melt butter. Add in 1 C flour, 1Tbs. sugar, vinegar and salt. Pat out into a tart pan with a removable bottom. Refrigerate while preparing the filling.

Mix together pippins, cinnamon, ½ C sugar and 1 Tbs. flour. Place in prepared crust, then dot top with butter. Bake 60 minutes at 350 degrees.

You can replace the filling with other fruit and substitute sugar for brown sugar. Sliced peaches laid out in a circle around the pan add a lovely look to the dessert.

Dessert

LEMON TEA MUFFINS

From Linda Jenkins

2 C flour
2 tsp. baking powder
$\frac{1}{2}$ tsp. salt
1 C margarine, soft
1 C sugar
4 eggs, separated
$\frac{1}{2}$ C concentrated lemon juice
$\frac{1}{4}$ C finely chopped nuts
2 Tbs. brown sugar
$\frac{1}{4}$ tsp. nutmeg

Combine flour, baking powder and salt. In a large bowl, beat the margarine and sugar until fluffy. Add the egg yolks and beat until light. Gradually stir in the lemon juice alternately with the flour mix. Beat egg whites until stiff but not dry. Gently fold $\frac{1}{8}$ of them into the batter, then gradually fold in the rest. Fill muffin tins $\frac{3}{4}$ full. Combine nuts, brown sugar and nutmeg and sprinkle on top. Bake 15-20 minutes at 375 degrees.

Makes about 18.

Dessert

DOUBLE BROWNIE PUDDING

From Ann Marra

1 C flour
2 tsp. baking powder
½ tsp. salt
½ C granulated sugar
½ C milk
1 tsp. vanilla
2 Tbs. shortening, melted
½ C semi-sweet chocolate chips
¾ C brown sugar
¼ C cocoa plus 2 tsp.
1¾ C hot water

Sift together flour, baking powder, salt, granulated sugar and 2 tsp. cocoa.
Add milk, vanilla and shortening; mix until smooth. Add chocolate chips.
Pour into greased 8-inch square baking pan. Mix brown sugar and cocoa;
sprinkle over batter. Pour hot water over the entire batter and do not stir.
Bake at 350 degrees for 40-45 minutes. Makes a chewy brownie top and
a rich pudding below. Serve completely cooled with a scoop of vanilla
ice cream.

Dessert

ORANGE ROLLS

From Mabeth Oxenreider

1 pkg. dry yeast
$^1/_4$ C warm water (105-115 degrees)
1 C milk, scalded
$^1/_4$ C sugar
1 tsp. salt
$^1/_4$ C vegetable oil
1 egg, beaten
About 3$^1/_2$ C all-purpose flour

Orange Butter – make this first
$^1/_2$ C butter softened
1 C sugar
grated rind of 2 oranges

Combine all three ingredients; beat at medium speed with electric mixer until fluffy. Makes 1$^1/_2$ cups.

Dissolve yeast in warm water, set aside. Combine milk, sugar and salt. Stir well and cool to lukewarm. Combine yeast mixture, milk mixture, oil and egg. Stir well. Add 1$^3/_4$ C flour and beat well. Stir in remaining flour. Beat well. Cover and let rise in a warm draft-free place until double. Punch down and divide in half. Turn out dough on a heavily floured board. Knead each half lightly 6-8 times to form two smooth balls. Place stockinette on rolling pin; flour well. Roll out each ball into a 14" x 9" rectangle. Spread $^3/_4$ C Orange Butter over each rectangle, leaving a 1" margin. Roll up rectangles, lengthwise. Pinch long edges to seal. Do not seal ends. Cut into 1$^1/_2$" slices. Place slices, cut-side down, into two well-greased cake pans, leaving $^1/_2$" between rolls. Rolls may be covered with plastic wrap and frozen at this point. If not freezing, cover and let rise 30 minutes or until double. If frozen, thaw and let rise until double. Bake at 375 degrees for 25-30 minutes or until golden. Remove from pan while hot. May be frosted with orange powdered sugar frosting* while warm. Makes 2 dozen rolls.

Orange Powdered Sugar Frosting – to a basic powdered sugar frosting, add orange juice as a liquid, and the zest of one orange.

Dessert

ORANGE PIZZAZZ

From Susie M. Robbins

½ C water
½ C orange marmalade
½ C sugar
½ C orange liqueur
14-20 oranges

In a small saucepan combine all ingredients except the oranges. Boil ingredients until they become a syrup (approx. 15 mins.).

While the syrup is boiling, cut 14-20 oranges in the following manner: With a sharp knife, cut all the peel and white pulp from the oranges. Section each orange into a bowl. When all the oranges are peeled and sectioned, drain the juice and set it aside for breakfast. When the syrup has cooled, pour it over the oranges and marinate overnight.

This recipe works wonderfully as a splash of color for a special breakfast or as a festive addition to a luncheon, especially when served in a crystal goblet. It is delightful as a light dessert served with a fancy cookie and a piece of chocolate. For an extra bit of "pizzazz," add a candied violet. Divine! What a treat for the eye.